THIS STORYBOOK IS PRESENTED TO:

The Kent Family

ON THIS DATE:

December 2021

PRESENTED BY:

The Santa Rosa Primary

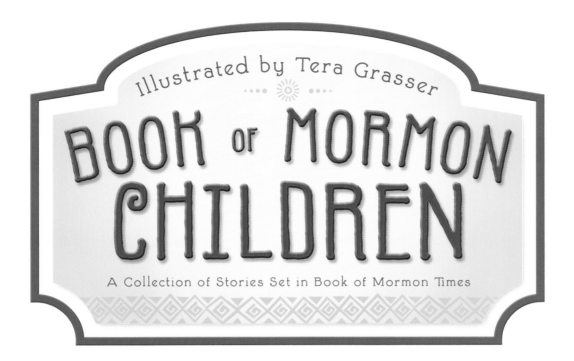

Illustrated by Tera Grasser

BOOK of MORMON CHILDREN

A Collection of Stories Set in Book of Mormon Times

Merrilee Browne Boyack

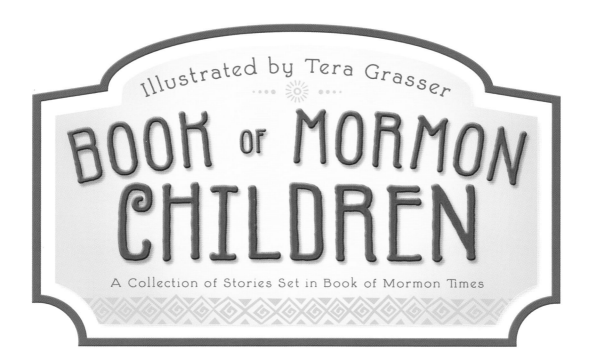

Illustrated by Tera Grasser

BOOK OF MORMON CHILDREN

A Collection of Stories Set in Book of Mormon Times

Merrilee Browne Boyack

Bonneville Books

An Imprint of Cedar Fort, Inc.

Springville, Utah

ISBN 13: 978-1-4621-1053-7

LIBRARY OF CONGRESS CATALOGING-IN-PUBLICATION DATA
Boyack, Merrilee Browne, author.
  Book of Mormon children : a collection of stories set in Book of Mormon
times / Merrilee Browne Boyack.
     pages cm
  Includes bibliographical references and index.
  ISBN 978-1-4621-1053-7
  1. Book of Mormon--Fiction. 2. Children--Fiction. I. Title.

  PS3602.O9235B66 2012
  813'.6--dc23

                            2011049314

Published by Bonneville Books, an imprint of Cedar Fort, Inc.
2373 W. 700 S., Springville, UT, 84663
Distributed by Cedar Fort, Inc., www.cedarfort.com

Cover design by Danie Romrell
Cover design © 2012 by Lyle Mortimer
Edited and typeset by Melissa J. Caldwell

Printed in the China

10 9 8 7 6 5 4 3 2

Printed on acid-free paper.

TO MY GRANDCHILDREN

MAY YOU COME TO LOVE
THE BOOK OF MORMON
AS MUCH AS I DO.

Contents

Contents

Contents

One

ANNA'S ANSWER TO PRAYER

And it came to pass that Anna, daughter of Sam and granddaughter of Lehi, awoke in her family's tent. She heard the birds chirping first. Within minutes, her mother rose and made her way out of the tent. Anna stretched her arms over her head and stuck her toes out of her blanket. Morning time was her favorite. Her mother stuck her head back inside the tent. "Anna, time to get up and milk the goat!"

"Yes, Mother," murmured Anna, stretching one last time.

She stood up slowly and ran a bristle brush through her long dark hair and quickly tied it into a braid. Anna was tall for her age and had deep brown eyes. She put on her tan dress and reached for the brown sash she usually wore. Her hand stopped. Today just felt like a special day. So she dug into her sack and pulled out the beautiful orange sash. Her mother, Anurah, and her father, Sam, had given it to her for her birthday. Her mother's hands were still orange from the berries she had used to dye the yarn.

Anna danced outside with the sash in her hands. Happily, she ran her fingers through the fringe at the ends of the sash. Then, seeing the goat looking at her, she tied the sash around her waist and went to work.

The morning passed quickly, and Anna finished her chores around the camp. It had been eight years since her father, Sam, and his brothers Laman, Lemuel, and Nephi and her mother's family of Ishmael had left Jerusalem. They were now camped in a land they called Bountiful beside the great sea Irreantum.

Anna had some free time in the afternoon, and she was curious. She had heard that Uncle Nephi had a forge in the mountain to make metal tools. Uncle Nephi and all the family were building a ship to take the family across the sea to a special land. The forge had a big fire that was used to heat the metal. Anna was very curious. She had not seen much fire.

She worked her way down the beach to the place where the ship was being built. The big, curved wood pieces stuck up in the air like a big skeleton. She found Uncle Laman and Uncle Lemuel napping under a tree nearby. "Uncles!" she called. "Is Uncle Nephi at the forge?"

"He went up this morning," replied Uncle Lemuel lazily. "He's probably still up there praying and trying to figure out what to do next. I still think this is crazy. He's never built a ship and this one is going to sink." Laman and Lemuel laughed at that, slapping each other on the back.

Anna slipped away and found a path at the bottom of the mountain behind their camp. She had been curious for a long time, and today was the day when she would see the big fire! She ran her fingers through the fringe on her sash excitedly. She didn't notice the little threads that fell out onto the ground. She walked up the path that became steeper and steeper. After a while, she looked between a clearing in the trees and back down the hill. She could see the camp far below and it seemed much smaller.

After a time, Anna could hear banging sounds. She climbed toward them. The shadows were getting longer and the trees darker. After a long time, she realized that the sounds were coming from across the steep valley on the other side of the mountain. She decided to turn around. Anna ran her fingers through the fringe on her sash nervously as she walked. After she had walked for a time, she realized that she was not sure which path to take. She tried one and then another.

Finally, she sat down. She was so tired. And she was lost. She didn't know which way to walk or which way to turn. Anna remembered that she had been taught that if she was ever lost, she should sit down and stay until she was found.

But it was getting dark. And it was getting cold. Anna heard some sounds that scared her. She wrapped her sash around her shoulders to keep warm. And she began to cry. Big teardrops ran down her long dark lashes. As she cried, she remembered her mother teaching her. "Anna, the Lord will always be with you. You can pray to Him whenever you need help."

Anna turned and knelt by the bottom of a big tree. "Heavenly Father," she started. Then she began to cry again. "Heavenly Father, I know that you are there and that you love me. Please help me, Heavenly Father. I'm lost and I'm afraid. Please help my father to find me."

Anna leaned back against the tree. She felt a warm feeling in her heart. She knew that Heavenly Father loved her and would keep her safe. Suddenly, a thought came to her mind, "Throw your sash into the tree."

Well, that's just silly! she thought. *I love my sash.* But after a minute, the thought came to her mind again, "Throw your sash into the tree." She said a little prayer. "Heavenly Father, am I supposed to throw my sash into the tree?" Anna felt that same warm feeling again.

"Well, here goes!" she said, tossing the sash high into the tree. It was like a bright orange line over her head. She sat down and wrapped her arms around her knees, shivering a little more now.

She fell asleep for a little while. But soon shouts woke her up. She could see torches down the path.

"Anna! Anna! Where are you?"

It was her father shouting.

"Father, I'm here!" she called.

Soon a group of men with torches was at her side. Her father swept her up and hugged her. "Oh, Anna, we thought we had lost you!" he cried. Her uncles, Nephi, Lemuel, and Laman, were patting her on the back. Anna hugged her father tightly.

"How did you ever find me?" asked Anna.

Uncle Laman held up his hand with a grin. "Well, you

left a bit of a trail." Anna gasped. Uncle Laman held orange threads in his hand.

"Oh!" said Anna. "They must have fallen out when I was playing with the fringe on my sash!"

"Yes, but then it got too dark to see the little threads," said Uncle Nephi. "But just as we were about to turn back, your father could see your sash in the tree. Why did you throw your sash in the tree?"

"I prayed to Heavenly Father, and I felt like I was supposed to," explained Anna.

"Well, it's a good thing," said her father. "We would have never found you without it!" He reached up high into the tree and pulled the sash down. "Now, where's my beautiful daughter?" he asked and spun her around, tying the sash around her waist. Then he scooped her up and put her on his shoulders. "And is my beautiful daughter ready to go home?"

"Oh, yes, Father!" Anna smiled. "Let's go home!" And as Anna rode home on her father's shoulders, she said a little prayer in her heart. "Thank you, Heavenly Father," she prayed. "Thank you for saving me and for loving me."

And it came to pass that Anna knew that her prayers had been answered and that she was never alone. And she patted her orange sash and knew that her parents loved her and that Heavenly Father loved her too.

LEARNING ACTIVITY: ANSWERS TO PRAYERS

- ☀ Every day this week, when you say your prayers, stay on your knees when you are done talking and listen. Wait a few minutes and think about your prayer, think about your Heavenly Father, and think about how you feel.

- ☀ Read 1 Nephi 17 and 18 to learn about Nephi's ship and the family's travels across the sea.

DID YOU KNOW?

- ☀ In Hebrew, the name *Anna* means "prayer."

- ☀ The Israelites raised goats called the Nubian Ibex. The boy goats have a little beard and so do the girl goats! The girl goats give milk just like a cow does.

Two

BENJAMIN LEARNS TO REPENT

And it came to pass that Benjamin, son of Joshua and Leala, who was the sister of Nephi, dug along the bottom of the creek with his fingers. "Ah, a good one!" he exclaimed and pulled out a smooth, round stone. He examined it closely. "This one is special!" he said as he noticed a red line running through the middle of the rock.

He added the rock to the small pile by the side of the creek. He climbed out of the creek and scooped up the small pile of rocks. What a fine collection he had! He had about twelve rocks: some gray, some black, two white ones, and now his special rock with the red stripe. All were smooth and round from being in the water.

Benjamin excitedly put them into the leather pouch that was tied at his waist. He scrambled up the bank of the creek and sprinted across the meadow. Soon he reached his village.

"There you are, my little rascal!" called his mother. "Where have you been?"

"I was collecting rocks," explained Benjamin.

"Rocks, rocks, rocks. You must have rocks in your head!" She laughed and rubbed his black hair that never seemed to lay flat. "It's time for your chores," said his mother as she carried the basket of grain toward the village.

"Yes, Mother," said Benjamin. He ran off to get the water pots. It was his job to get fresh water for the family. He had forgotten to take the water pots along in his excitement to gather new rocks.

Benjamin worked quickly, filling the water pots and gathering sticks for the fire. He fed and watered the animals and helped his father cut wood for the family to use.

Soon it was time for the little children to take their naps. But Benjamin was too excited to sleep. He snuck out of his tent and walked quietly to the edge of the village.

Ah, trees! Benjamin's favorite thing to do was to throw rocks. He threw rocks at big rocks. He threw rocks over the edge of the big hill at the other end of the village. He threw rocks into the creek. But he loved to throw rocks at trees most of all. He would pick a spot on the tree and try to hit that spot with his rock.

The men in the family had slings to throw their rocks, but Benjamin was still too young to have a sling. He was just as happy throwing rocks.

He had heard the story of David and the giant Goliath. He had learned how young David had killed the giant with his sling and his rocks and saved the Israelite nation. Benjamin wanted to be the best rock thrower ever so that when he got a sling, he would have the best aim of anyone.

Benjamin saw a skinny tree and threw a few rocks at the dark spot on the tree. Ping—ping! The rocks hit the target easily.

Benjamin walked on looking for harder targets. Up the path, he saw the temple on the hill. He walked toward the large building.

Uncle Nephi and the men of the family were building a large temple. He had been told that it was like the temple of Solomon back in Jerusalem, but he didn't quite understand that. It was the biggest building he had ever seen.

Oh, but look! There was something new! A tall column of

wood was in front of the temple. It stood so high, Benjamin had to shield his eyes from the sun to see it all. It was as tall as two men!

But what was really special was what was on the wood. Carved up and down the front of the wooden pillar were many big circles, one after another. *Zoram must have carved them*, thought Benjamin. Zoram was a great woodcarver.

Benjamin stared up at the big carved circles on the tall pillar of wood. And a thought came to his mind. "Oh, they're the perfect targets!" said Benjamin. And before he could think another thought, he backed up and began to throw his rocks at the circles.

Over and over and higher and higher, he threw his rocks. As he would go to pick them up, he noticed little dents in the wood pillar. But he ignored them and kept throwing his rocks.

After a long time, he grew tired and walked over to a tree beside the temple and curled up to take a nap.

"Hey, sleepyhead!" Someone was nudging Benjamin with his toe. "What are you doing here?"

Benjamin looked up to see his Uncle Nephi standing over him. "Oh, I couldn't sleep and came here," said Benjamin, and then he shut his lips tight.

His Uncle Nephi sat beside him. "Well, I can't think of a better place to take a nap. This is a sacred place. We will finish building the temple today and tomorrow we will dedicate it to the Lord."

"What?" asked Benjamin.

"That is when I will say an important prayer, and then this temple will be the House of the Lord. It will be His house and always a sacred place for our people. We will worship the Lord here," explained Uncle Nephi.

"You mean it's really God's house?" asked Benjamin. "Is He going to live there?"

Uncle Nephi chuckled. "Well, yes, in a certain way. This is where we can be with Him and worship Him. He lives in Heaven, but this will be one of his special houses on our land. It will be His temple."

Benjamin felt terrible. "Why the sad face?" asked Uncle Nephi.

"Oh, nothing," said Benjamin. "I'd better get back." He rose slowly and walked down the hill.

As he walked, Benjamin felt heavier and heavier. *What have I done?* he thought. He didn't feel like going back to his home and turned to the woods. He sat by the creek. *I have been throwing rocks at God's house*, he thought, *and I left dents in that beautiful pillar in front of the temple.* Benjamin felt so sad.

Soon, great tears welled up in Benjamin's eyes and he began to sob. "Oh, what have I done? That was so bad," he cried. After a time, he stopped crying and thought, *What can I do now?*

Then Benjamin remembered that his father had taught him about repentance. His father had said, "If you do something that you know is wrong, you need to repent. You need to say you are sorry and then try to fix whatever you did wrong. Then ask Heavenly Father to forgive you and He will."

Oh, thought Benjamin, *I am so very sorry.* So he knelt in the soft sand by the creek and prayed. "Heavenly Father, I am so, so sorry about throwing rocks at the temple. I should never have thrown them at Thy house. And I feel so bad about leaving dents. I will never throw rocks at things that can be hurt ever again. Please forgive me." Benjamin cried a little bit more. "Please forgive me, Heavenly Father. I will try to be a good boy from now on."

Then Benjamin stood when he was done praying. He felt a little bit better. He walked toward the temple. As he walked, he felt better and better. He reached the big wooden pillar. He looked up at the pillar and felt a little sad again.

Zoram stood by his side. "Wonderful, isn't it?" he asked, placing his big hand on Benjamin's shoulders.

"Oh, yes, it is beautiful," said Benjamin. "And I am so very sorry."

"But why?" asked Zoram. Benjamin walked over to the giant pillar and ran his hand softly over the small dents.

"I threw rocks at the pillar," whispered Benjamin softly. "And I feel really bad about it."

Zoram's hand rested on his shoulders again. "Would you like to fix it?" he asked.

"Oh, yes!" exclaimed Benjamin. "Can I?"

Zoram smiled and handed him a small tool. "Just take this and move it over all the dents and they will go away."

Benjamin began to work, smoothing all the dents in the large pillar. After much time and effort, he stood back to look at his work. "I can't even see them," he said.

Zoram came over and stood by his side. "Good work, Benjamin. I'm proud of you. I would like to teach you more about woodcarving if you would like to learn."

"Oh, yes, I would. Thanks!" replied Benjamin.

The next day the family all gathered around the temple. Nephi asked them all to be seated, and he began to pray.

As he prayed and talked to the Lord and asked Him to accept the temple that they had all worked hard to build, Benjamin felt a sweet peace in his heart. He knew that the Lord had forgiven him. "Oh, thank you!" he whispered in prayer to his Heavenly Father.

And it came to pass that Benjamin had learned that repentance helped him feel better and that he could fix his mistakes. He had learned that Heavenly Father would forgive him if he would repent. Benjamin peeked up at the tall beautiful pillar in front of the temple. And he felt happy.

LEARNING ACTIVITY: REPENTANCE

※ Every day this week when you say your prayers, think about your day. Did you do something that was wrong and you feel bad about? Go through the same steps that Benjamin did and repent. Try to fix anything you can and say you are sorry to anybody you have hurt. Then ask the Lord to forgive you. When you do, think about how you feel.

※ Read 2 Nephi 5 to learn about Nephi building the temple in the Book of Mormon.

DID YOU KNOW?

※ The name *Benjamin* means "favorite son."

※ Two circles next to each other, like the number 8, make a symbol that means "eternity" or "forever." Our temples make us forever families.

Three

CARMELINA AND CALEB CHOOSE HONESTY

And it came to pass that Caleb and Carmelina, son and daughter of Jacob, grandchildren of Lehi, begged their mother. "Please, Mother, can we go fishing now? We've finished all our work and it's late in the afternoon. Please, can we?" Caleb made his brown eyes very big, and Carmelina twirled her long dark blonde hair in her fingers.

"Oh, you two!" said their mother, laughing. "Just be careful and don't be gone too long." The twin brother and sister grabbed a small woven basket and skipped toward the river.

"Race you to the river!" cried Caleb as he dashed across the meadow. Carmelina happily ran after him, finally beating him to the creek edge. "You are too fast," said Caleb. He went over to the small tree by the creek edge and pulled on a rope that was tied there. Soon a small raft made of tree logs and rope came closer to the edge.

The two children climbed onto the raft and carefully placed their basket with the fishing net inside. Caleb reached over and grabbed a long pole that had been leaning against the tree. "Let's go!" he said.

Brother and sister took turns pushing with the long pole and moving the raft up the river. Luckily, the river was very slow at that time of the day, and they easily worked their way upstream. Finally, they reached their favorite fishing place and tied the raft to a nearby tree.

The children slipped into a quiet pool of water by a big rock at the edge of the river. They each held two corners of the fishing net and let it sink to the bottom of the water. They stood very quietly.

After a time, three shiny fish swam in between them. "Quickly!" called Caleb and both children snapped their hands together and up into the air. There, squirming in the middle of the net, were the three shiny fish. "We caught them!" laughed Carmelina. They carefully carried the net with the fish to the raft.

"I'll get them in," said Caleb, and he grabbed the fish and put them in the basket, putting the lid on quickly and placing a rock on top to keep the basket shut.

They caught another fish a short time later. Then, after a much longer time, two more.

Finally, both children were tired and lay on their raft, dangling their toes into the water. "Let's hope the fish won't bite our toes!" said Carmelina, laughing.

"You silly," said Caleb. "What's that?" he whispered, sitting up suddenly.

"What are you talking about?" replied Carmelina.

"I can hear voices," whispered Caleb. "Keep your voice down!"

"Now, David, I know that you're a smart man. How can you believe in this story about a Christ?" a tall man spoke.

"Well, my parents taught me that He would come," replied another man.

"Well, how do they really know?" the tall man spoke again. "I believe what I can see and read."

Carmelina and Caleb looked at each other. There were several men on the bluff above the river talking. "I don't think we should be here," whispered Carmelina nervously. "Let's go home." Caleb picked up the long pole and gave a gentle push on the river bottom. Soon the raft began to float down the river.

When they were far from the bluff, Caleb spoke up. "I don't understand what those men were arguing about."

Carmelina answered, "I remember Father talking about a man who doesn't believe that Christ will come. He is telling people false things. Father says that the man is evil."

"We'd better tell Father what we heard," said Caleb, and Carmelina nodded her head.

After some time, Carmelina called out, "Caleb, look!" Caleb looked where she pointed. On the river bank, by a rock, was a small leather pouch. Caleb reached over with his long pole and managed to snag the pouch. He pulled it back carefully to the raft.

He held the pouch out for Carmelina to see. "Look at this!" he said. He opened the pouch. Inside were several gold coins. "Look at all this gold!" he exclaimed.

"Who do you think it belongs to?" asked Carmelina.

"It has a big 'S' on the front," said Caleb. "Let's take it to Father and see if he knows whose gold this is."

The two children reached their starting place and quickly

tied up the raft. Grabbing the pouch and their basket of fish, they ran up the riverbank and across the meadow to their village. It was getting to be very late, and they could see their mother lighting the lamps.

"It's about time!" she called out to them. "I had to save you some dinner. Did you catch some fish?"

The children quickly handed her the basket of fish and ran past her to their house. They dashed inside the door and just as quickly ran out. "Where's Father?" they asked.

"He's up the street at the village well," replied their mother. The children ran past her, with Caleb clutching the leather pouch.

"But wait!" their mother called, but the children did not hear.

As they approached the center of the village, they stopped short. There was their father, Jacob, and there was a group of men standing in front of him. "Show me a sign!" demanded the tall man. The children gasped.

"That's the same man!" said Caleb. "I recognize his voice."

"They must have come back here while we were getting the pouch," said Carmelina. "It looks like they're arguing."

"If God shall smite thee, let that be a sign unto thee that he has power, both in heaven and in earth; and also, that Christ shall come. And thy will, O Lord, be done, and not mine," said their father in a powerful voice. Just as he said those words, the tall man dropped to the ground like he was dead.

The children ran to their father. "Is he dead?" asked Caleb.

"No, son," replied Jacob, their father. "But Sherem has done bad things and needs to learn about the power of God." The men surrounding him were shocked to see what had happened. Jacob turned the children away as the other men picked up the tall man and carried him away.

"Why are you here?" asked their father. The children quickly told their story and showed their father the pouch and the gold coins. "It has a big 'S' on it so it must belong to Sherem," said their father. "We'll take care of this later." Their father put the pouch into the pocket of his robe. "Come, children, it's late and you need to eat and get to bed."

After several days, their father took them to bring food to Sherem. He was in a bed and was very weak. As Jacob went to Sherem with some food, Sherem sat up in his bed. "You are kind to come," said Sherem. He smiled at the children. "Thank you."

"The children have found something they think might

be yours," said Jacob. He pushed the children forward.

Carmelina held out the pouch. "Is this yours, sir?" she asked. Sherem smiled sadly.

"Yes, that is mine. Thank you for returning it to me." The children bobbed their heads and backed to the door.

Sherem handed the pouch to Jacob. "Jacob, I have been an evil man and I am sorry. Take this gold and give it to help the poor."

Jacob took the pouch and put it in his pocket. "I will, Sherem."

The next day, the children asked their father what had happened to Sherem. "He had done very bad things, and he needed to tell the people the truth. He told all the people that Christ was real and would come and that he had been wrong. And then he died," said their father sadly. The children felt very sorry.

"But I am grateful that I have honest children who helped him do some good," their father said as he hugged them both.

And it came to pass that Carmelina and Caleb were glad that they had been honest. They were so happy that they had returned the pouch with the gold coins and that now the money would help the poor.

LEARNING ACTIVITY: HONESTY

☀ Play the "What If?" Game with your parents. Have your mommy or daddy ask you questions to see if you know what to do to be honest. Here are some examples:

☀ "What if you found a wallet on the sidewalk? What would you do?"

☀ "What if you really, really wanted some candy at the store but didn't have any money? What would you do?"

☀ "What if you didn't pick up your toys and your mommy asked you if you did? What would you do?"

☀ "What if your brother had a dollar on his desk and you really wanted to buy a toy? What would you do?"

☀ Your mommy or daddy can make up some more questions to play the game with you. They can help you if you're not sure what you should do.

☀ Read Jacob 7 to read about Jacob and Sherem.

DID YOU KNOW?

❋ In Hebrew, Carmelina means "little garden" and Caleb means "brave."

❋ In Book of Mormon times, the fishermen used nets, spears, and hooks to catch fish to eat. You can read about Peter in the New Testament who was a fisherman. When he met Jesus, Jesus told him to go fishing again and he caught so many fish, his nets broke! You can read about it in Luke 5.

Four

DANIEL'S FAIR FOOTRACE

And it came to pass that Daniel, son of Amaleki, darted among the tents and tables. "Catch me if you can!" he cried as he ran off across the field.

"Wait, wait!" cried his little brothers and sisters as they scrambled to keep up with him. But Daniel ran ahead, his dark wavy hair bouncing as he ran.

"There he goes again," Amaleki chuckled. "I think that boy is part deer and part rabbit!"

Daniel's mother smiled as she opened the baskets of food. "Well, he gets it from you, you know. You don't sit still very much either," she replied. "He wants to be just like you were—the fastest runner in the whole area."

Amaleki raised his hand in greeting to the man approaching their tent. "Greetings, Samuel."

"Greetings, Amaleki. It's going to be a great day," the man replied.

"Yes, it is," answered Amaleki. "What a good idea to have a celebration of the whole land of Zarahemla. It is such a wonderful blessing that we were all led away from the Land of Nephi so that we could be safe. The Lord has truly blessed us and the people of Zarahemla have been so kind to let us join them."

"Yes, this is truly a great day of celebration," agreed Samuel. "Is that boy of yours ready for the big race?"

"He will be if we can ever catch him!" Amaleki laughed.

Daniel soon caught up with his friends. "Hey, Seth, have you seen the jugglers?" he asked.

Seth, a big boy wearing his best striped gray tunic, pointed. "We're heading there now."

The boys and girls soon gathered around the two men who were juggling. The first man tossed three red, shiny apples round and round in the air. The second man tossed two logs, over and over, up and down. Pretty soon the first man tossed an apple to the second man. He caught it and tossed a log back. Then the two men began tossing apples and logs back and forth as the children laughed and clapped.

The men then tossed the apples to some of the children, who began to try and juggle as well. Everyone laughed together as the children kept dropping the apples. "Don't worry," said the first man. "It just takes practice."

The children wandered off to the other booths to see all the exciting things happening. One older man sat on his blanket telling stories to everyone gathered nearby. He told of the great voyage in the ship when Lehi brought his family across the ocean. Then he told the story of how Mulek had led his people across the ocean as well and how the Lord led both groups of people to be there in Zarahemla that day.

Then the young friends came to a woman handing out big pieces of warm bread spread with honey. They smacked their lips and licked their sticky fingers after eating the delicious bread.

As the day wore on, a large group of people gathered. Mosiah, the king, stood on the large platform. "Greetings to all," he said. "We have been having a wonderful day together. But now I think we have a very important event.

Are the children ready for the footrace?" All the children cheered.

Soon all the children had gathered at the starting point. Daniel was bouncing up and down—he was so excited. Daniel was a thin boy, with long straight legs. He loved running more than anything, and he was very, very fast.

It was time for the race to begin. Amaleki stood on the platform. "Now remember, everybody stay on the main path. Is everyone ready?" The children and their parents cheered. "All right then. Ready, set, go!"

At just that moment, Daniel yelled at the children. "Hey, everybody! Look over there!" He pointed to the side of the starting line. All the children waited and looked. Daniel took off running as fast as he could, laughing.

"Haha! I tricked you all!" he called and ran ahead of the children. Soon they began to run after him. Along the path, they all ran. Turning here and there, following the turns in the trail, the children ran on, with Daniel far in the lead.

"Ah, here is the shortcut I found!" Daniel said to himself as he ran. He turned into the trees and soon was running and jumping over branches, rocks, and tree roots. He darted up the narrow path, dodging this way and that.

"Where did Daniel go?" asked a girl as she came around the turn on the main path.

"He must be ahead of us and around the corner," replied another girl with her braids bouncing as she ran. "Let's run faster and try to catch up to him." On they went.

Daniel was just about done running along the shortcut. At last, he saw the main path and turned right, sprinting along the way. "Ha-ha! The others are way behind me!" he laughed. "They didn't know about the shortcut." Daniel ran around the final curve of the path and could see the finish line with all the parents gathered. When they saw Daniel coming, everyone cheered him on.

Daniel whizzed past the finish line with a big smile on his face. His father and mother were cheering for him. "You won! You won!" they cried. Everyone was patting him on the back and congratulating him. After a while longer, the rest of the children came running to the end and soon the race was over.

"It's time for the award," called King Mosiah. "Everyone gather." Daniel and his parents walked up to the platform. "Now, Daniel, as winner of the race, you get this big shiny medal." The king held up the shiny medal on the bright red leather strap.

Amaleki grabbed Daniel's hand and raised it into the air. All the people cheered. But as Daniel looked at the other children, he got a lump in his throat. He pulled his hand down. He tugged on his father's shirt. "Father?" he said quietly. Amaleki turned to his son.

Daniel stepped forward. "I do not deserve this medal," he said. "I didn't race fairly." The crowd was quiet. "I knew a shortcut, and I didn't stay on the path."

King Mosiah turned to Daniel. "Daniel, you have done a brave thing telling the truth. Thank you." Daniel hung his head.

"Now my people. The day is still young. Why don't we have another race that's fair for everyone and see who can run the fastest?" All the people cheered. Soon they were lining up all the children again. The King pushed Daniel toward them. "Now, Daniel, you made a mistake. Why don't we try this again and you be fair, all right?" Daniel nodded his head.

He walked up and down the line of the children and shook each of their hands. "I promise to race fairly this time. Is that all right with you?" All the children shook his hand and said yes.

Amaleki raised his hand. "Get ready, set, go!" he yelled.

Off went all the children together. They ran and they ran. All along the path they ran, with Daniel running as fast as he could. As they neared the finish line, Sarah, with her braids bobbing, crossed the finish line first. Daniel was close behind.

"Good job, Sarah," said Daniel as he hugged his friend. "You were very fast today." Sarah smiled.

And it came to pass that Daniel felt good about himself and how he ran the race. He had been fair this time and had obeyed the rules. He learned that playing fair was more important than winning. And he knew that he would practice his running all year long so that he could be faster in the race the next year.

LEARNING ACTIVITY: FAIRNESS

※ This week, pick out a game to play with your family. Have your family go over all the rules to the game. Then play the game together and keep all the rules so that you play fairly. Have fun playing the game, whether you win or not.

☀ Read the Book of Omni in the Book of Mormon to learn about the people of Nephi finding the people of Zarahemla. Ask your mother and father this question: Where did the people of Zarahemla come from?

DID YOU KNOW?

☀ The name *Daniel* means "God is my judge."

☀ Runners were used to carry information between villages in the times of the Book of Mormon. In ancient Greece, they had a big race every four years from 776 BC (that's 176 years before Lehi left Jerusalem) until about 400 AD (that's about when the Book of Mormon ends). This race in Greece was the first Olympic games. You can read about the Olympics and the runners we have today at your library.

Five

ELIANA LOVES HER FAMILY

And it came to pass that Eliana, daughter of Mosiah, granddaughter of King Benjamin, wrapped the blanket more tightly around her shoulders. It was going to be another long night, she thought. She could hear her mother moving in the other part of the room.

"Oh, Mosiah, it's no use. I just can't get any sleep," Eliana's mother, Abigail, sat up in her bed, rubbing her back stiffly. She stood slowly, her big belly pushing against her robe. Her mother twitched. "Oh, this baby is kicking me in the tummy again. He may be small, but he's sure strong!"

The next morning, Eliana quietly climbed out of her bed, careful not to wake her mother, who had fallen back asleep. She got dressed quietly and went out to tend to the animals that needed watering and feeding.

Her father greeted her. "How is my best girl?" Eliana smiled up at him. "I do believe that you missed a spot when you washed your face this morning," he exclaimed. Then he swept her up in his arms and flipped her upside down. Holding her there, he looked over her. "Yes, there it is! You missed a spot on the bottom of your chin." He reached under her chin and tickled her.

She wiggled in his arms. "I did not!" she protested.

"Well, all right . . ." said her father. With that, he flipped her around and set her on her feet, laughing.

"Mother is still sleeping," she said.

"Thank you for getting up and helping with the chores," replied Mosiah. "I must go to the fields on the other side of the village. Do you think you could watch over your mother today?" he asked.

"Of course," said Eliana. Her father tickled her under her chin and kissed her forehead.

"Thank you, sweetie," he said and gathered up his pack.

Eliana went back into their house and went over to the

fire. She poured the water into the large pot and swung it over the fire. Then she went to the table and began to cut up some fruit.

"Good morning, dear," called her mother. "Come help pull me out of the bed. I am so big, I think I'm stuck in this bed forever."

Eliana laughed and went to help pull her mother up. She helped her mother to a chair. She had tied her long dark blond curls behind her head with a scarf and had folded her mother's apron in half and put it on. "Breakfast is ready!" she exclaimed and gave her mother some bread, fruit, and a hot grain drink she had made for her.

"My, my. I could get used to this!" said her mother as she ate hungrily.

The day wore on and Eliana worked hard to take care of the house and her mother. Her father came home and greeted his little family. "How is everyone here?"

"Well, I think I might be out of a job if Eliana keeps this up," replied her mother.

After supper, the family gathered around the small fire as it grew dark. Suddenly her mother sat up. "Oh, my!" she exclaimed. Her face looked very pale.

"What's wrong?" asked Mosiah.

"I think the baby is coming," said her mother in a frightened voice.

"But it's not due for over a month," said Mosiah.

"Oh, owww," was all her mother could say. She groaned. "I think something is wrong."

Mosiah and Eliana helped Abigail to the bed to lie down. She moaned and groaned and tossed back and forth on the bed. "I don't like this," said Mosiah as he wiped her forehead with a damp cloth. "I think I better go get Anna, the midwife. The midwife will help your mommy have her baby. Can you take care of your mother for a time?" he asked. "I'll hurry."

"I'll do my best," replied Eliana.

After a time, Mosiah returned with the midwife. The midwife went to Abigail to check on her. She returned. "That baby is coming now, and it doesn't look good," she said. "I need clean cloths and hot water." Eliana scurried around the house, getting Anna the things she needed.

The birth of the baby was very difficult, and Eliana was scared watching her mother. After a while, the tiny baby was delivered and wrapped in a cloth. "It's a boy," said Anna, the midwife. "A very *tiny* boy. We shall have to pray that he lives. You take the baby to your father now. I need to tend to your mother," said the midwife, handing the small bundle to Eliana.

Eliana looked down into the eyes of her tiny baby brother. His dark eyes looked up at her from the little red, wrinkled face. "Hello, little brother," she said. "I'll take care of you." She took the baby over to see her father. "Look, Father, he's beautiful."

"Yes, he is," Mosiah replied. "A fine son. Let us pray to the Lord that he will be all right—and your mother." His worried face looked past her to her mother and the midwife.

The midwife finished her work and Abigail slept. "Your wife is very weak," she said to Mosiah, "and I'm sorry to say the baby is not much better. Feed your wife broth and soft food, if she'll eat it. I'm afraid she's too weak to feed the baby. But I delivered a baby down the street a few weeks ago to Miriam, and I'm sure she will help you feed your baby. That is all we can do. Now I must leave you because another baby is coming soon on the other side of the village. Good luck to you."

Mosiah slumped to a chair. "Whatever shall we do?"

"I will help, Father. Do not worry. We love Mother and this little boy and so does the Lord. He will bless them both," said Eliana.

Mosiah rubbed her head. "My little Eliana, you are so faithful and brave and have so much love."

And so the next few days were very difficult. Every day, Eliana took her baby brother, whom her father named Ammon, to Miriam down the way to be fed. She took care of the house and cooked for her mother. She changed the swaddling cloths for her little brother so that he would stay clean and dry. Late at night, when he was fussy, she would walk and walk as she held him, singing to him softly. Her father would help care for her mother and the baby as well.

After over a week had passed, Abigail was much stronger. She sat up in bed. Mosiah came in and sat beside her. "You look better today," he said.

"I'm feeling a little better," she replied. "What have you been doing this morning?"

"I've been telling all the people in Zarahemla that my father, King Benjamin, is going to make a big speech to everyone in the land in two days. He will be making me king of the land. He has asked us all to gather at the temple. He wants a tower to be built so that he may speak to all of us."

"Well, we must go," his wife replied.

Mosiah looked at her with alarm. "You can't go! You're not well enough."

"I can lay in a tent just as well as in a house," she replied. And so the little family got ready to set up a tent by the temple. A low bed was made for Abigail to lie on.

And early in the morning, King Benjamin climbed the tower to speak to the people. Eliana was thrilled to see her grandfather standing so high. He spoke of Jesus Christ and how He would come to earth, heal the people, and bring the truth. Then he told the people, "Believe in God. Ye must repent of your sins. And if ye do this ye shall always rejoice and be filled with the love of God." He taught them for a long time. He also taught the parents what to teach their children: "Ye will teach them to love one another, and to serve one another."

Eliana looked down at her very tiny little brother, Ammon. "I *do* love you!" she whispered. "I have served you for almost two weeks now. I love you so much that my heart could break." A little tear slid down her cheek as she snuggled her brother. And then a sweet feeling of peace came to her, and she knew that her brother would live and that all would be well.

Her mother called to her. "Eliana, come sit next to me."

Eliana sat down. "You have been so kind and helpful to me and to your little brother. Thank you for all you have done. Now I know why you have the special name you have. Your name means 'God answered me.' When I was younger, I prayed and prayed that I could have a baby and then you came. I know that God answered my prayers and that you have answered my prayers now by helping us. I love you, sweetheart."

And it came to pass that Eliana had learned to love by serving those she loved best. She had felt the love of Jesus Christ in her heart. And she knew that He loved her and her family too.

LEARNING ACTIVITY: LOVE

☀ Every day this week, give your mom and dad and brothers and sisters a big hug and tell them that you love them. You could even do helpful things for them to show them. If you would like, you can make little love notes for everyone in your family. Have your mommy or daddy help you cut out some hearts and you can color on them and put them on everyone's pillows.

☀ Read Mosiah 1–6 to read about King Benjamin's great talk from the tower in front of the temple. Ask your mommy and your daddy what happens to Ammon when he grows up. (Hint: He becomes a great missionary!)

DID YOU KNOW?

☀ The name *Eliana* means "God answered me."

☀ The families in the Book of Mormon cooked their food over fires or in large ovens. They ate lots of vegetables, beans, lentils, cucumbers, onions, and lots of bread. For meat, they would eat a little fish or lamb and hunted in the forests in America for other things to eat. They also liked honey because it was sweet.

Six

GUR'S FAITH
BECOMES STRONG

And it came to pass that Gur, son of Helam, sat on a rock. This was a pretty good rock, as rocks go. It was just big enough and had a nice flat spot on the top where Gur could sit comfortably. And the back of the rock was higher so it was almost like a little chair.

"Here I sit, like a king!" said Gur.

His brother turned and laughed. "Well, excuse me, oh noble king. I hate to interrupt, but I do believe one of your loyal subjects is escaping." Gur looked past his brother and saw a medium-sized sheep trying to walk quickly away from the herd. He jumped up from the rock.

"Hey, you, get back here!" Gur cried and ran after the sheep. The faster Gur ran, the faster the sheep ran. Finally, he took a giant, flying leap and tackled the sheep. The sheep bleated loudly. "No use complaining," said Gur as he herded the sheep back to the rest of the herd.

"Nice capture," said his older brother. "Do you always have problems with sheep staying in your kingdom, oh king?" He bowed deeply at his brother and came up laughing.

"Oh, be quiet," muttered Gur.

Gur was short and couldn't run very fast. But he had a big smile and large green eyes. His reddish-brown hair was very wavy and seemed to never stay in the same place.

Gur and his brother Reuben were tending the sheep. Actually, his brother was only going to be there for a few more days and then would leave for the village. His other brother who was just older than him, Jasher, would be coming next. It would be Gur's first time alone tending the sheep.

The sheep were another story. Some were very nice and very obedient. And some were rather ornery and always trying to escape. But they all needed water, and they all needed nice grass to eat. So Gur led them to the creek each day to drink and up to the meadow to eat.

The days passed, and it was time for Reuben to leave.

"Now be careful, little brother," he said. "If a wild animal comes, you just beat your sticks and then run to the cave where you'll be safe. Jasher will be here very soon." And off walked Reuben with his pack over his shoulder, whistling.

Gur sat on his rock. Then he led the sheep down to the creek very carefully. Not one tried to escape. Then he led them back to the meadow and sat on his rock again. After a while, he was very bored and began to doze off.

"Hello there, young man," said an old man standing in the sun. Gur woke up with a start.

"Who are you?" he asked.

"That depends on whether I can trust you or not," replied the old man.

"My father says that I am very trustworthy," said Gur.

"Well, then, my name is Abinadi," said the old man.

"What are you doing all the way out here?" asked Gur.

"Would you like to hear the story?" asked Abinadi. "Or are you busy?"

Gur laughed. "Oh, I'm terribly busy right now watching sheep eat grass. But maybe you could tell me a short story."

Abinadi sat on the ground in front of the rock and leaned back. "Well," he began. "I am hiding from King Noah."

"What!" exclaimed Gur as he jumped up from his seat.

"It's all right," said Abinadi. "I am not a bad man. I am a prophet of God."

"Oh," said Gur.

Abinadi then told Gur that he had been called of God to tell the wicked King Noah and all his evil followers that they needed to repent. He told about going through the city of Lehi-Nephi commanding the people to repent because they had been doing bad things.

"I bet they didn't like that," said Gur.

"You're right," said Abinadi, and he chuckled softly. "Now the king wants to kill me."

"Oh no!" exclaimed Gur.

"And so I am hiding," said Abinadi. "I have been hiding for two years. But soon I must go back and preach to the people again."

"Well, I know a great hiding place," said Gur. Gur took Abinadi and showed him the dark cave in the hill. "See, you can't even see it from outside because of the trees and rocks."

"May I stay here a while?" asked Abinadi.

"Of course," said Gur.

And so Gur and Abinadi spent several days together, talking and watching the sheep. Abinadi taught Gur all about the Lord and about the commandments.

"My father doesn't like King Noah," said Gur. "He says he's a bad man and that the taxes are too high."

"Yes, but do not be too sad," said Abinadi. "I don't think King Noah will be bothering the people too much longer."

One day, Gur could hear his brother Jasher from far away. "Quick, that's my brother coming," said Gur. "You better go hide in the cave."

"I will," said Abinadi. "But in the morning I must go to the village. The Lord has told me that I must tell the people to repent or terrible things will happen to them."

"Oh, please be careful!" said Gur. Abinadi just smiled and patted his shoulder.

"Remember, Gur, always have faith in the Lord and you will be protected." Abinadi gathered his pack and moved off toward the cave.

Jasher came up over the hill. "Hello, brother!"

"Hello, Jasher!" called Gur. He asked his brother all about the family and what was happening in the village.

"Well, I see that you've tended the sheep very well," said Jasher. Gur smiled. "Father wants us to bring the sheep back to the village," said Jasher. Gur was surprised. "We must go early in the morning," explained his brother.

The next morning, the two brothers began the long task

of herding the sheep back to the town. After two long days, they arrived outside the town where their family lived. They herded the sheep into the large pen and went inside the house.

"Welcome home, boys!" called their mother. "Hello, sons!" called their father, Helam. As the boys sat, their parents began to tell them of what was happening in the city. "That old prophet Abinadi has returned," explained Helam. "He is telling the people to repent."

"Well, I agree with him," said their mother. "The people do not worship the Lord as they should and haven't kept the commandments." Gur felt good that his parents believed Abinadi.

The next day, all the city of Lehi-Nephi was in an uproar. "What is happening?" asked Gur.

Helam answered, "Abinadi the prophet has been speaking to King Noah and his wicked priests. He told them they must repent and stop being bad. They have taken him and thrown him in prison." Gur felt so sad.

He went quickly into the house and gathered up some bread and vegetables and a small bag of water. Out of the house he ran and down the street to the edge of the village. There was the prison. He crept around the back and called at the window in a loud whisper, "Abinadi, are you there?"

Abinadi's face appeared at the window. "Little Gur, what are you doing here?"

"I heard what happened and brought you some food and water." He handed up the bundle of food and the bag of water to Abinadi.

"You dear boy," said Abinadi. "Thank you."

Just then two prison guards walked around the side of the prison. "And what is this?" one of them snarled and grabbed Gur by the back of his tunic, lifting him into the air. "And what are you doing here, you little rascal?" asked the other, looking very scary.

"I came to help the prophet," said Gur, jutting out his chin as bravely as he could.

"Oh, and do you believe this so-called prophet? Should we throw you into jail with him?" Gur trembled. He did believe the prophet. He believed in the Lord. But if he said so, he might be thrown into prison.

Just then Gur remembered Abinadi's words telling him that he should always have faith and he would be protected. Looking the dirty men in the eye, he said loudly, "Yes, I do! I believe everything he has said. And you should too!" Then Gur held his breath.

The prison guard holding him looked him in the eye

closely. "Well, if that doesn't beat all. This is a strong little one, after all. What's your name?"

"My name is Gur," he replied.

At that the man dropped him to the ground and began to laugh. "Gur? Your name is Gur? Ha ha ha. That means 'young lion.' Well, you sure have a big roar today!" The other man began to laugh and soon the two were bent over laughing and slapping each other on the back.

Gur looked up at the window. He could see Abinadi smiling at him. "Never lose your faith, young lion. You will be strong and mighty someday. No matter what happens, always have faith in the Lord." Abinadi turned from the window.

Gur quickly moved away from the prison and ran home.

And it came to pass that Gur had learned that having faith in the Lord was the most important thing he could do. He had learned that the Lord would always be with him as he had faith in the Lord. And someday, he would serve the Lord like Abinadi.

LEARNING ACTIVITY: FAITH

☀ Ask your mommy or daddy if you can put a picture of Jesus in your bedroom. Every day look at that picture and think about Jesus and all that He has done for you.

❃ Read Mosiah 11–17 to read the story of Abinadi. Have your mommy or daddy show you the picture of Abinadi preaching to King Noah.

DID YOU KNOW?

❃ The name *Gur* means "young lion." Doesn't it sound like a young lion when you say it?

❃ A person who tends sheep is called a shepherd. The shepherd's main job was to keep the sheep safe from harm. When David in the Old Testament was tending his sheep as a young man, he killed a lion and a bear that tried to attack the sheep. When Jesus was born, angels appeared to the shepherds who were tending their flocks and they went and were the first visitors to see the baby Jesus. One of Jesus's names is "Shepherd" because he keeps each of us safe from harm. Gur learned that the Lord was his Shepherd and kept him safe too.

Seven

HANNAH GETS BAPTIZED

nd it came to pass that Hannah, daughter of Alma, held the lamb more tightly. The lamb wiggled and baaed miserably. "It's all right, you poor dear," said eight-year-old Hannah to the lamb. "You're just getting a haircut. You'll feel much better when this is all over." The lamb still struggled.

"Keep a firm hold on her," said her father, Alma. He worked carefully and quickly to cut off the lamb's woolly coat. The wool fell in big clumps as he trimmed. "There, now. All done," said Alma.

Hannah let go of the lamb. The lamb, free of its heavy

wool coat, jumped about. Hannah laughed. "There now, you skinny thing. Don't you feel a lot cooler?" The lamb darted off, baaing for its mother as it joined the other trimmed sheep of the herd.

"You can gather up all that wool for yourself like I promised," said Alma. "You've done a good job caring for your lamb. Now it's time for you to learn to weave its wool. What will you make?"

"I haven't decided yet," said Hannah, scooping up the piles of wool into her apron.

"Well, I know it will be special," said Alma. He turned to the next big sheep with his tools.

Hannah skipped back to her house. "Mother, mother," she called. Her mother, Rebecca, stood at the table in front of their house. "Look at all the wool I got from my lamb!" Hannah opened her apron, dumping the wool on the table.

"Well, well. That lamb must have been more skinny than we thought!" her mother replied. "It sure had a big woolly coat."

Mother and daughter carefully worked to clean the wool. After it had been cleaned, Rebecca got out her tools. She showed Hannah how to carefully stroke the wool with the two bristle paddles. "This will straighten out the wool and get it ready for spinning," she said. Hannah was very excited to learn how to weave and listened carefully to all of her mother's directions.

The next day, Hannah was up early. She quickly finished her work and then followed her mother around as she worked. "All right, all right," said her mother. "It's time to spin." Her mother got out the round spindles. She showed Hannah how to spin the round wood spindle in her one hand and to place the strands of wool onto it. As it went round and round, the strands of wool began to join together until a string of yarn began to form. Mother and daughter worked over the next few days getting all the wool spun into long loops of wool yarn. As they worked, Hannah dropped things less and less and began to work faster and faster. At last, all the yarn was done and looped and tied.

"Now what?" asked Hannah.

"Well, you get to pick a color," replied her mother.

"Yellow, bright yellow!" exclaimed Hannah.

"I'm not surprised," said Rebecca. Hannah's favorite color was yellow.

"Then we need to make some yellow dye to color the yarn," said her mother. "You will need to go to the riverbed and gather some of that bright yellow moss. Why don't you take your little brother with you?"

Hannah gathered up a small pot and took her brother, Alma, by the hand. "Come along, Alma, and don't get into trouble." Little Alma looked up at his sister.

"I won't," he promised. Hannah rolled her eyes. Alma the Younger always seemed to be getting into trouble. Her mother had told her that that was what little brothers are supposed to do, but Hannah wasn't so sure.

The two children walked to the river's edge. They began to flip over rocks. "Ah, here's some good moss growing on this rock," said Hannah. She got a stick and began to scoop the bright yellow moss into her pot. As she was digging, she heard voices.

"I have heard that Alma preaches that we need to repent and follow the commandments," said one woman with a blue scarf on her head.

"Yes, I heard him last night as he taught," replied the other woman as she scrubbed the clothes on a rock. "I had such a good feeling as he spoke and taught us about the Lord and the scriptures."

"Yes, but King Noah is very angry. It's so dangerous to listen to Alma," said the first woman.

"King Noah is wicked, and we all know it," replied the woman washing. "I love how I feel when I listen to Alma. I'm going to follow him, no matter what happens."

Hannah was happy to hear that the woman believed her father. It had been scary since that day when her father, Alma, had come home and told the family that he believed the prophet Abinadi. Her father had had to hide much of the time since then because of the wicked king. Even now, the family was very careful. Alma had been teaching the people quietly and many more were following him.

Hannah and her brother returned to their home. Their parents were sitting at the table. "I got some moss to color the yarn," said Hannah. She set down her things and sat by her parents. "And I heard some women talking about you, Father, by the river." Hannah told her parents what she had heard.

"That is good," said her father. "I have been praying, and the Lord has now told me that our followers need to be baptized. We need to show the Lord that we are willing to follow Him and we will do that by being baptized."

"Won't that be dangerous?" asked Hannah.

"Yes," replied her father. "But we will do what the Lord tells us to do."

For the next few days, Alma and Rebecca talked quietly to the people and told them of the plan. Finally, it was late in the day. Alma had been hiding in a group of trees. Rebecca and Hannah walked along the river, stopping and watching to make sure they were not followed. Finally, they reached the waters of Mormon. It was a pool of pure water, surrounded by rocks and trees.

"Are we sure that no wild animals are here now?" asked Hannah nervously.

"Let's just hope they are gone today," replied her mother. They sat on a rock and watched as more small groups of people came quietly, all of them looking over their shoulders and all around. Finally, over two hundred people were gathered.

Alma stood and spoke to the people. "I am happy to see all of you here," he said. "We know that our lives are in danger from King Noah and his army. But we also know that the Lord lives and that we must follow Him. We must have faith in the Lord no matter what happens to us." The people nodded their heads.

Alma then stood at the water's edge. He asked the people if they wanted to become the people of the Lord. "Now I say unto you, if this be the desire of your hearts, what have you against being baptized in the name of the Lord, as a witness before Him that ye have entered into a covenant with Him, that ye will serve Him and keep His commandments?" All the people clapped their hands and said this was what they wanted to do.

Then Alma went into the water with his friend, Helam. He said those important words, "Helam, I baptize thee, having authority from the Almighty God," and both Alma and Helam went under the water. They came up and hugged each other tightly.

From then on, Alma did not go under the water but took each person by the hand, led the person to the water, and baptized him or her. Finally, all of them were baptized. Alma made his way out of the water to the rock where Hannah sat.

"Hannah?" he said. "Would you like to be baptized?"

"May I?" asked Hannah.

"Do you believe in the Lord?" he asked.

"Oh, yes! Yes, I do," replied Hannah.

"And are you willing to help others and to keep God's commandments?" he asked.

"Oh, yes. I will do my very best," replied Hannah.

"Then I believe that you are ready," said Alma.

He gently took Hannah by the hand and led her into the waters of Mormon. "Hannah, I baptize thee, having authority from the Almighty God." And with that he slowly lowered Hannah into the water until she was completely under the water and brought her up again. Hannah smiled a big smile, and her father grabbed her in a big hug.

"Oh, thank you, Father," she whispered. "Thank you."

"I am proud of you," said Alma. "This is not an easy thing, but we know it is right," he said. He led her back to her mother, who wrapped her in a blanket.

Alma turned to talk to the people. "We do not know what will happen after this night," he said. "But we do know that as of today, we are the people of the Lord. We will follow Him and do as He commands us, and He will be with us." Then all the people quietly walked away in small groups, talking in low voices.

And it came to pass that Hannah was grateful that she had been baptized. She knew that it was the right thing to do because she loved the Lord. She wanted to keep his commandments all her life and this was an important beginning.

LEARNING ACTIVITY: BAPTISM

☀ Ask your parents to have a family home evening to talk about baptism. Ask your mom or dad to tell you about when they were baptized and how they felt. If your mom or your dad was a missionary, have them tell you about the people they taught while on their mission. Talk with them about when you will be baptized and what you need to do to get ready.

DID YOU KNOW?

☀ The name *Hannah* means "merciful."

☀ In the Book of Mormon times, people made cloth from weaving wool yarn. They also collected cotton that grew in America on cotton plants. They would color the cloth with dyes made from flowers, moss, leaves, rocks, or nuts to make all different colors.

Eight

ISAAC HAS HOPE

And it came to pass that Isaac, son of Simon and Mary, scrambled out from between the bundles. "Hey, what are you doing? Get back here, you rascal!" yelled one of the Lamanite guards. Isaac ran as fast as he could, laughing. He dodged around the corner and leaned against the wall to catch his breath.

"Playing with the guards again?" boomed a deep voice. Isaac jumped.

"Oh, Uncle Jeshua, it's you," he whispered. "You scared me!"

"Good!" chuckled his uncle. "You're playing a dangerous game with dangerous men."

"They can't catch me," bragged Isaac. "I'm too fast for them."

"Be careful, little one. Now you get home. It's growing late." Isaac's uncle gave the small boy a gentle shove.

Isaac walked slowly through the town. His reddish-brown hair waved around his ears. Isaac had taken a lot of teasing over those ears that stuck out from his head. He had short legs and a small body and looked like his dad. He saw his mother lighting the lamps in his home. He loved this time of day when the family gathered. He and his family lived in the city with the people of Limhi. The Lamanites ruled over the people and they were treated like slaves. The people had been praying to the Lord to help them become free. At night, safe in his home, Isaac felt safe and warm. He hoped that their prayers would be answered.

"Would you like some bread and cheese?" asked his mother as Isaac sat in the corner of their small home.

"Yes, please," answered Isaac. He quickly ate and then picked up his bundle of rope-making supplies. Isaac loved to make rope. He would gather twine and dried plants wherever he could find them. In the evenings, he would sit and twist and weave them into strong rope. He finally had a very long rope that he was very proud of.

"Shall we put that rope to good use tonight?" asked his father.

"What do you mean?" asked Isaac.

"I have been gathering medicines and plants and herbs," replied his father, Simon. Isaac's father was a healer—like a doctor—and helped to keep the people healthy.

"What for?" asked Isaac.

"I know that our prayers will be answered and somehow we will escape," replied his father. "I've been gathering medicine to prepare. Your cousin, Moshe, is hiding in a cave outside the city. He has been gathering many things to help us prepare for our escape. I need to get these medicines to him and your rope will be a big help."

Isaac was excited. He gathered up his rope and his father tied the medicines, plants, and herbs into a basket.

Off they went quietly into the night. They quietly made their way to the city wall. "Now, Isaac, help me tie the rope through the basket handles." They tied it very carefully. Then his father tapped on the wall three times with a rock. Isaac could hear three quiet taps from the other side. They lowered the basket of medicine quickly. After a few minutes, they pulled back the rope and it was empty. Three more taps from the outside of the wall and they knew Moshe had the basket and would hide it in the cave.

Isaac and his father repeated this for several nights. After a week had passed, it was again evening time and there was a quiet knock at the door. Two men came quickly inside. Isaac recognized Gideon, a strong man who helped protect the city, and Ammon, the missionary who had come to the city and taught the people about Jesus Christ and the gospel. "Simon, we have important things to talk about," the two men said as they sat and talked to Isaac's father. "We have a plan to escape from the Lamanites." Gideon then explained that they were going to give wine to the Lamanite guards who guarded the city gates and kept the people of Limhi trapped. "They'll fall asleep and we will escape."

"How can I help?" asked Simon.

"Well, we will be traveling with all the people and we're worried that we'll need medicine. Can you gather all you have and be ready to go in two days?"

Simon leaned back his head and laughed. "It's already been done!" he exclaimed.

"What?" asked Gideon. Simon explained how he and Isaac had been lowering medicines over the wall and how

Moshe had hidden many things in the cave outside the city. "Well, how about that!" Gideon slapped his knee. The men finished talking about the escape and then said good-bye to the little family.

"Do you think we'll really be able to escape?" Isaac asked his father. Simon put his hands on Isaac's shoulder.

"We always have hope that our prayers will be answered," Simon replied. "Always keep that hope in your heart."

The next couple of days were busy as the little family packed their belongings. Soon the night came. The family moved through the streets with their sheep and cows. Their belongings were strapped on their donkey. They had used Isaac's long rope to tie on the bundles holding all the things they would need. All the families of the city were gathering at the back side of the city. After a time, the signal came as Gideon stood upon the wall swinging his lamp from side to side. The people moved as quietly as possible. After leaving the city, they quietly walked around the camp of the Lamanites.

Isaac had to clap his hand over his mouth to keep from laughing out loud. The Lamanite guards were drunk, and they had all fallen asleep. Isaac giggled because he could hear the guards snoring loudly. Their snoring was so noisy!

No wonder they couldn't hear the people or animals quietly walking by.

After a long time of walking, they came to the edge of the wilderness. They were long past the guards. King Limhi stood on a large group of rocks. "Hear me, my people! Our prayers have been answered. The Lord has blessed us and we have escaped from the Lamanites. We must move quickly so that their armies cannot catch us. But I wanted to stop now and offer a prayer of thanks to the Lord for helping us." All the people kneeled down. Ammon, the missionary, stood next to King Limhi and said a prayer to the Lord, thanking Him for helping the people to escape. All the people said, "Amen!" and then quietly kept walking. It would be a long night.

Isaac was feeling sleepy. His father picked him up. "Are you tired, my little one?" he asked.

Isaac nodded. "But, Father, I am so happy that we are free."

"Yes, we are finally free!" agreed his father.

"I had hope just like you said," replied Isaac. "I hoped our prayers would be answered and they were."

"Yes, little one. Our hopes have come true. Now, why don't you ride on the donkey for a time?" Isaac stretched himself out over the bundles on the donkey, winding his hands into his long rope to hang on, and promptly fell asleep.

And it came to pass that it had been an exciting night for Isaac and his family and all the people. He had learned that if you hope for what is right, you will be blessed. Now his family and his people were free.

LEARNING ACTIVITY:
HOPE

☀ For family home evening, have everyone in the family write a list of all the things they hope will happen to them when they grow up. Keep your list someplace safe and read it often. You can pray and ask Heavenly Father how you can help make those good things happen!

☀ Read Mosiah 22 to find out what happened to King Limhi's people. Find out the name of the city where they went to be safe.

DID YOU KNOW?

☀ The name *Isaac* means "laughter."

☀ The people in Book of Mormon times used rope to help them move things and store things. They made their rope from plants they found growing in the area. They also made twine, which is like a strong string. To help them carry a bigger load, they also used what is now called a "tumpline," which is a strap (a type of sling) along with a rope. The strap—made of plant fibers or of leather—went over the forehead. Then the person tied the rope to a net or to other things such as a water jar.

You can find this picture at http://manderson
.home.igc.org/teacherguide2/lesson2.html.

Nine

JOEL
CHOOSES OBEDIENCE

And it came to pass that Joel, son of Joash, brother of Alma, grabbed the wiggly fish with both hands. "You've got a lively one there!" called his father. Joel took the fish over to the big basket by the rock and put it carefully inside. "Well, that should be enough for the party tonight," his father said. Joel helped Joash gather up the nets and baskets with the fish inside.

The son and father walked back to their village as the sun rose higher in the sky. Joel was a small boy with wiry brown hair and small, bright brown eyes. He had bushy eyebrows that his brothers and sisters teased him about all the time.

He was small but strong, and he helped his father carry the baskets full of fish back to their home.

"We're home!" called Joash to his family. His wife, Elena, was small and dark like her son, and she came quickly over to help her husband lift the baskets to the tables.

"You certainly caught a lot this morning!" she said, laughing. "Did you empty the river?"

"Oh, no, mother," replied Joel very seriously. "We left a few that got away." His parents chuckled.

"Are Sam and Aaron tending to the animals?" Joash asked.

"They're not up yet," replied Elena. "They were up very late last night with their friends."

Joash's face grew dark. "They're always out late with their friends," he said in a low voice. "It's time they paid attention to doing their work." He went to the tent where Joel's older brothers slept. "Get up, both of you! Get to work!" Joel's brothers slowly came out of the tent with tired eyes and scowling faces.

"What's the big rush?" complained Aaron.

"Yeah, why do we have to get up so early?" asked Sam.

"We're having a party today for Grandfather's birthday," explained their mother. "Did you forget?" Both boys grumbled and moved off to care for the animals.

"Those boys have been trouble ever since they started spending time with Alma and those four sons of Mosiah," said Joash with a frown.

"I know," agreed his wife. "They've been going around trying to tell people that the Church isn't true and causing all kinds of problems."

"I'm worried about our sons," said Joash as he put his fishing gear away. "They have been getting meaner and meaner."

Elena wiped a tear from her cheek quickly. "What can we do?" she asked.

"Let's pray some more," said Joash. "Alma has asked all of the members of the church to pray for his son and for the sons of Mosiah."

"That took great humility for Alma to ask for that," replied Elena. "Many of us are having problems with our children."

Joel listened to his parents quietly. He felt sad that his older brothers were causing problems and making his parents worried and upset.

"Joel, would you help me clean these fish?" asked his mother.

"Yes, Mother," answered Joel, and he got the scraper and

the knife. He watched as his mother cleaned and scraped the fish. Joel liked scraping the scales off the fish. It was a little tricky, and it had taken him quite a while to learn how. But now he was getting faster. Scrape, scrape—off came the shiny scales that caught the light of the sun. Soon the fish were smooth and ready for cooking.

"You've been working hard all morning," said his mother. "Would you please help me with one last thing? Then you can go play for a while.

Will you take this money to Rahab the baker and ask her to deliver the extra bread tonight at sunset for the party?" She gave Joel several coins, which he tied in a cloth and fastened at his waist. "Don't lose that money," his mother reminded him. "We need that bread for the party tonight."

Joel scampered down the way with his wiry hair bouncing with each step.

Through the village he went. Soon he saw his brothers by the village well, arguing with a group of people. "How do you actually *know* that Christ will even come?" one of the sons of Mosiah called out.

"Yeah, you can't prove anything your church teaches," called out Joel's brother Sam. Joel tried to quietly slip past the people.

"Ho there," said his brother, catching him by his shirt. "And where are you going?" he asked his little brother.

"I have to give this money to the baker," answered Joel. His brother tried to snatch the money from his hand, but Joel held tight onto the small pouch.

"Give me that money!" said his brother angrily. "I want to get something sweet, and Father never gives us any money."

"I can't," replied Joel. "Mother told me to give it to the baker."

"You give it to me, or I'll give you a beating," threatened his brother. At that, Joel darted out of the way and his brother began to chase after him. Joel ran as fast as he could and managed to hide behind a barrel until his brother gave up chasing him. Then he went a different way until he had found the baker's shop.

Joel gave the baker the money and carefully went around the village well on his way back. He went off to play with his friends in the field outside the village.

Later in the day, he returned home to find his mother and sisters busily working on getting the food ready for the party. "There you are, little one!" she said. "Did you have fun playing?"

"Yes, Mother," he replied.

Just then they heard shouting up the street. Soon they saw several men carrying a young man. Several people were surrounding them and there was a lot of talking. "What has happened?" Elena said to her son.

"I don't know," Joel replied.

"Isn't that Sam and Aaron?" said his mother as the group came closer. Joel hung back behind his mother in case his brother was still angry with him.

The young men came closer. "Sam, Aaron, what is going on?" called out their mother. Sam and Aaron came over to her.

"Something strange has happened," Sam said. "We were walking out of town and came across Alma the Younger and the four sons of Mosiah. They were all lying on the ground."

"It was so strange," said Aaron. "They were all just lying there with pale faces. We helped to wake up the four brothers, but Alma is still in a strange way. It's like he's asleep or something."

"What happened to them? Were they attacked?" asked Elena.

"No, the sons of Mosiah said that an angel of God appeared to them," answered Sam.

"A what?" exclaimed their mother.

"They said it was an angel—all dressed in white and surrounded by bright light."

"What did the angel say?" asked Joel in a timid voice.

"Well, they claim that the angel told them they had to repent and quit saying bad things about the church. He said many people were praying that they would repent and be good again," answered Aaron.

Elena and Joel looked at each other. "Do you believe them?" asked Elena.

"We don't know what to believe," said Sam. "But we are taking Alma home to his father to see if he can help him." Sam and Aaron walked off with their friends to carry Alma the Younger to his home.

Joash came up from the field. "What was that all about?" he asked. His family told him all that had happened. "This is truly an answer to prayers," exclaimed Joash. "How did Aaron and Sam feel about it all? Did they believe them?"

"They're not sure," answered Elena, "but they know that something *did* happen. There's no doubt about that."

"Then let's hope that they too will repent and be obedient once again," said Joash.

Later that night, the whole family and their friends gathered together for their party. Everyone was talking about the angel and the young men.

Sam came up quietly to his parents. "Mother, Father, I'm sorry about how bad I've been these past few months."

He hung his head and spoke quietly. "I know I haven't been obedient, and I've caused you a lot of worry." His parents gathered him in a hug. Then they stood back.

"How does Aaron feel about all of this?" they asked.

Sam hung his head again. "He doesn't really believe it. He's been arguing with Mosiah's sons all afternoon." Elena's eyes filled with tears. "I'm sorry, Mother. I should have never taken him with me to meet with my friends."

She squeezed his hand. "We know you're sorry."

"All we can do at this point is pray for him," said Joash. "Our prayers have been answered this day, and I believe they will be answered again to help us save Aaron."

Sam walked away and saw Joel sitting on a long bench. He sat beside his brother and patted his head. "I'm sorry, little brother," he said. "I was very mean to you today, and I'm really sorry. Will you forgive me?" Joel hugged his big brother. "Joel, I'm proud of you. You have always been a good obedient boy and you do what you're told. You've always been a good example to me. I'm going to try harder to be a good example to you." Joel felt a warm feeling in his heart.

And it came to pass that Joel knew that choosing to be obedient was always the best thing he could do. He had seen the sadness that came from choosing to be disobedient and he saw that being obedient made people happy. He knew that he would always try to be an obedient boy.

- ❋ Play Simon Says with your family for Family Home Evening. Ask your mom or dad if you can keep a sticker chart this week and get a sticker for each time you are obedient and do what you're told.

- ❋ Read in Mosiah 27 to find out what happens to Alma the Younger and the four sons of Mosiah.

- ❋ The name Joel means "God is willing."

- ❋ The people of the Book of Mormon often built their cities by rivers and by the ocean. The people were able to get a lot of food from the water, including fish, shrimp, and a pasta-like food called ahuatle. From the ocean they ate crabs, oysters, fish, and turtles. All these foods helped the people to be healthy and strong. Have you eaten any of these things?

Ten

KESHET LEARNS TO BE PATIENT

And it came to pass that Keshet, daughter of Eunice, threw the rock very quickly. It hit the lake and skipped over the water. "Aha! Seven skips! Beat that!" She clapped her hands and laughed to her friend, Adiella.

"I give up!" her friend laughed back. "You are truly the Queen of the Lake!" Then she leaned down and splashed Keshet.

"Wait a minute, you two," called out Eunice, Keshet's mother. "We're here to work, not play."

"Aw, Mother, all we do is work!" said Keshet, frowning.

"I know, but we should be grateful."

"I am," mumbled Keshet as she moved to help her mother.

Keshet was a tall, thin girl with long arms and long legs. Her golden hair hung straight to her waist. She wore a brightly colored headband to hold her hair back. Her tan-and-gold dress was tied at the waist with a braided colorful band of fabric. She bent to pick up the bundle of clothing near her feet and carried it to her mother.

Keshet and her mother lived in in a small hut on the outer edges of the city of Zarahemla Her father had died when she was a young girl, and she and her mother had to work very hard to take care of themselves. They washed the clothes of the rich people in the city.

She watched her mother take the clothes out of the bundle and dip them in the lake. Keshet helped her mother rinse the clothes carefully and then smack them on the water again and again to loosen any dirt that might be in the fabric. After they finished rinsing the clothes, they moved to the rocks by the edge of the lake.

Eunice was very strong and smacked the clothes on the rocks. Then back to the lake they went to rinse the clothes out so they were very clean. "Why does this always take so long?" complained Keshet. "Can't we just rinse the clothes once like everyone else?"

"You must learn patience," answered her mother. "It always takes time to do your best."

Eunice and Keshet took each item of clothing and wound it around and then squeezed as much water out as they could. Then they piled the clean clothing on the rocks. When they were done, they took turns spreading out the clothing on the grassy area to dry. When the clothing was dry, they would carefully fold each item and bundle up each family's wash. It was hard work that took up most of the day. At the end of the day, they would go to each house and deliver the cleaned clothing. They did not make much money but at least they would have enough to eat. Eunice and her daughter had worked hard, and the rich people of the city liked them and felt they did a good job washing their clothes.

As they walked tiredly to their little home, they walked past a group of women and their daughters. "Look at my new dress!" exclaimed one girl as she twirled around in front of the others. "It is made of fine silk and cost my father a lot of money!" All the girls and women clapped their hands. Gold and silver bracelets on their arms made a tinkling sound.

"Well, my new necklace cost far more than that!" bragged another girl with dark hair braided down her back.

Just then one of the girls saw Eunice and Keshet. "Euuwww," she said. "There's the poor washer woman. Let's walk on the other side of the road." And with that the group moved quickly to the other side of the road.

Keshet began to raise her fist to shake it at the women, but Eunice grabbed her arm. "Don't do it, Keshet."

"But mother, they're making fun of us because we're poor," she answered angrily.

"I know," said her mother. "But we must be patient with others. They are wrong and need to learn to do what is right. We must not react with anger."

Keshet wasn't happy about it. Tears stung at her eyes. She felt so sad that the other girls had made fun of her because she was poor. But she kept quiet as they walked home.

The next morning, Keshet and her mother worked especially hard and found that they were done by the late afternoon. They sat on the rocks for a minute to rest. "Mother, look!" The morning had been a little bit rainy but now the sun was shining through the clouds. There over the lake was a beautiful rainbow. "A rainbow!" cried Keshet. "I am sure good things will happen to us today."

Eunice patted her daughter's head. "You are the best thing that ever happened to me." She smiled.

The mother and young daughter delivered all the cleaned clothes and then wandered to the center of the city. There was a large group of people gathered and talking. Eunice and Keshet joined the group.

They saw Alma, the high priest, standing on the steps of the temple talking to the people. He wore a simple brown robe with a striped cloak. He spoke in a loud voice.

"And now behold, I ask of you, my brethren of the church, have ye been spiritually born of God? Behold, are ye stripped of pride? Is there one among you that doth make a mock of his brother?"

Keshet tapped her mother's shoulder. "Those girls and ladies we passed last night sure had a lot of pride! And they were mocking us and making fun of us! I wish they were here listening."

"Quiet, Keshet. We need to listen to the prophet for ourselves," whispered her mother.

Keshet began to listen more.

"The Lord God saith, come unto me and bring forth

works of righteousness. Whatsoever is good cometh from God. Will ye persist in the wearing of costly apparel and setting your hearts upon the vain things of the world, upon your riches?" said Alma.

Keshet certainly agreed with Alma that those things were bad.

But Alma continued, "Will ye persist in the persecution of your brethren, who humble themselves and do walk after the holy order of God, having been sanctified by the Holy Spirit, and they do bring forth works which are meet for repentance?"

Keshet suddenly began to think about herself. Had she been humble and patient with others? Had she been doing good things like the prophet talked about? She realized that she could be better too.

Alma talked for a long time and as he spoke, Keshet had a warm feeling in her heart. After he was done talking, a girl came up to her and reached out her hand to her. Keshet saw that it was the same girl with the long dark hair braided down her back—the one with the beautiful necklace. She took a step back away from the girl.

"Wait, please, I need to talk to you," said the girl. "What is your name?"

"My name is Keshet," Keshet replied softly.

"My name is Yoanna," said the dark-haired girl. "I must tell you how very sorry I am."

Keshet looked at her in surprise.

"I am a member of the church too, but I have behaved badly. My family used to be poor and I remember how hard it was. My father recently got a good job and is making a lot of money. He bought me this necklace and it was the first really nice thing I ever owned. I was bragging about it yesterday. But then I was so mean to you and your mother. Will you please forgive me?" Yoanna had tears in her eyes.

Keshet gulped and looked at her mother. Her mother nodded.

"Of course I will," said Keshet.

"I would like you to be my friend," said Yoanna. "Would you and your mother please come to our home for dinner tonight?"

Keshet and Eunice looked at one another and Eunice spoke, "We would be happy to."

With that, Yoanna gave Keshet a quick hug and told her where to meet. Then mother and daughter walked slowly home. "Mother, I believe the things the prophet said."

"I do too," replied Eunice.

"I know that I need to be more patient with other people," said Keshet.

"Yes, sometimes people take time to change. And sometimes we need time to change as well," answered her mother.

"Well, I am going to be patient with myself as well!" said Keshet.

"And with our work?" asked her mother.

"Yes, and with our work too!" said Keshet as she skipped home.

And it came to pass that Keshet learned that it was good to be patient. She had made a new friend that day and knew that she would be more patient from then on.

LEARNING ACTIVITY: PATIENCE

☀ Pick any of the following things to do that take patience and do at least one this week:

- Sit and watch the sunset. Sit quietly and watch the beautiful colors.
- Put together a large puzzle that takes

you a long time.

- Play a game with someone in your family that takes a long time to play.
- Make something that takes you longer than a day to finish.
- Sit quietly through a whole sacrament meeting!

☀ Have your parents read to you Alma's whole speech in Alma 5 and explain it to you. Alma asks many good questions to help us see if we are being good.

DID YOU KNOW?

☀ The name *Keshet* means "rainbow."

☀ In some countries of the world, the women still wash their clothes in a river, lake, or ocean. Aren't you glad you have a washing machine!

Eleven

LIRAZ IS KIND

And it came to pass that Liraz, daughter of Eli and Sarai, tossed the ball of dough high into the air. Her baby sister clapped her hands and laughed. Liraz caught the ball and began to pound it again on the table. Her sister laughed even harder.

"Keeping your sister happy?" asked her mother, Sarai.

"Yes, that's easy," replied Liraz. She pushed back the strand of hair that fell in her eyes.

"Well, you're turning into an old woman while you do it," laughed her mother.

"What!" asked Liraz with a shocked face.

"Your hair is turning white from all the flour," explained her mother.

Liraz had jet-black hair and jet-black eyes. Her long bangs kept falling out of her green headband and were now white and gray with flour. Liraz stopped and brushed her hands swiftly on her dark green dress. Then she flipped her long hair forward and back and tied it better with her headband. "There. Now maybe it'll stay in place!" she said to her mother.

Her sister clapped some more. "You'll just laugh at anything, won't you, my little Noya?" Liraz picked up her sister and danced her around the room. "Now I'm not the only one who's covered in flour!" She laughed as she danced with the baby. She placed her gently back on the bed. "Now I have to finish pounding this dough to make bread."

"You're really doing well on that loaf of bread," said her mother. Liraz was very proud that she was learning how to make bread. It was fun to pound the dough and fold it over, but it was hard work to get it to turn out just right.

"Yeah, maybe this loaf won't be hard as a brick!" called out her brother.

Liraz turned just in time to catch him dashing in the house and dashing out. "Well, you won't be getting any if you make fun of me!" exclaimed Liraz to her brother's back as he ran out.

Liraz and her family were Lamanites. They lived in the Land of Ishmael ruled by King Lamoni. Her father, Eli, worked for the king and was responsible for all of his horses and chariots.

Her father came home to eat lunch with the family. "Something strange has happened to the king," he told his family. "You remember I told you about Ammon, the Nephite?"

"The Nephite!" said Liraz's mother with a frown.

"I know, I know," said Eli. "We thought all Nephites were terrible, but I have to say, I am impressed with Ammon. He has been tending the flocks of the king. He saved the king's flocks from being scattered by the other Lamanites. The other servants told the king how Ammon had saved the flocks."

"How could he do that?" asked Liraz. "None of his other servants could protect the sheep."

"Well, that's just the point. No one has been brave enough or strong enough. King Lamoni thought that Ammon was the Great Spirit because of what he did," answered Eli.

"The Great Spirit!" exclaimed both Liraz and Sarai.

"That's how I felt," replied Eli. "But the servants said that Ammon said he was not the Great Spirit. But he said he was sent by God who is the Great Spirit and had much to teach King Lamoni and his people."

"And the king believed him?" asked Sarai.

"It seems so. The servants said they talked for a long time. Then King Lamoni prayed to God the Great Spirit and then fell to the ground," said Eli.

"Was he dead?" asked Liraz.

"Well, no one is really sure," he replied.

"What do you mean no one is sure?" asked his wife.

"He doesn't appear to be injured or sick. But he won't wake up. They carried him to the queen," he replied. "She is very worried about him. Liraz, would you go help the queen tomorrow? She is upset and you always cheer her up."

"I'd be happy to go, Father," answered Liraz.

The next day, Liraz went to the queen. "I am here to help, my queen," she said as she bowed low. "How may I help you?"

"Oh, Liraz, it is always so good to see you. Thank you for coming," replied the queen. All day Liraz helped the queen. She sang to her and played games with her and told her about her baby sister. She knew the queen was worried and hoped to help pass the time better.

The next day, Liraz went to help again. She washed the

face of the king and brought grapes to the queen. She even brought her baby sister for a time to help the queen feel happy.

On the third day, she was visiting with the queen when the queen began to cry. "I am afraid that my husband is dead. It is now the third day and still he does not wake up. Who can help my husband?"

Liraz had been thinking about this quite a bit. "Oh, queen. I have an idea. This Ammon, the Nephite, appears to be a man of great power. He was able to save the king's flocks. And I hear that his words are great. Maybe you could ask him to come and help?"

"What a good idea, Liraz! I shall call him at once," answered the queen, and she stood and rang the big bell. A servant came quickly.

"Go to Ammon, the Nephite, and ask if he will come to me," she commanded and the servant quickly left. After a time, the servant returned with Ammon behind him.

"How may I help you, oh queen?" asked Ammon as he bowed.

"The servants of my husband have made it known unto me that thou art a prophet of a holy God, and that thou has power to do many mighty works in his name. Others say that my husband is dead and that he stinketh but as for myself, to me he doth not stink."

Ammon smiled. "He is not dead, but he sleepeth in God, and on the morrow he shall rise again; therefore bury him not." The queen believed his words.

All night long the queen and Liraz watched over the king. The next day at the time Ammon had said, the king arose from his bed. He was alive! He was so happy!

"I have seen my Redeemer!" he said. Then he was so happy and the queen was so happy that they both fell to the floor.

All the servants were so surprised! They were also scared that something bad had happened. But as they prayed, they also fell to the ground because they felt the joy of the Lord. Even Liraz had prayed and had felt a strong feeling.

Now one of the Lamanite servants was a woman named Abish, and she had loved the Lord for many years. She ran to gather the people to see this wonderful thing.

Many people gathered and saw the king and queen and Ammon and the servants all lying down on the ground. They thought that maybe they had all been killed by Ammon because he was a Nephite. Some thought that Ammon was the Great Spirit. They were all arguing.

Then Abish went to the queen and touched her hand, and the queen woke up and jumped to her feet. "O blessed Jesus!" she cried. Then she touched her husband, and the king jumped to his feet. He saw the many people and that they were arguing. He told them the wonderful things he had learned. He touched Ammon, who then came to his feet and they helped all the servants to their feet and Liraz.

Liraz knew now that Jesus was her Lord, and she believed all the words that the king and Ammon preached to the people. Many of the Lamanites believed in the Lord and wanted to do what was right.

As the people left, the queen hugged Liraz. "Oh, my dear, you have been so kind to me! You have helped me so much these last few days and how I thank you! I don't know how I could have made it without you. Thank you so much for your kindness." She hugged her again and then took off her beautiful gold bracelet and put it on Liraz's arm.

"Oh, my queen, you are too generous! I am happy to help and you don't need to give me anything," said Liraz.

"I know," replied the queen, "but this is not only to thank you but also for us both to remember this great day and how we have learned about Jesus our Lord. Our lives will be filled with joy now." She hugged Liraz again.

"I must go to my parents and tell them what has happened," said Liraz.

"You hurry home and tell them I shall come to visit them tomorrow," replied the queen.

Liraz ran all the way home and found her mother and father sitting at the table in their home. She excitedly told them everything that had happened. Her parents were very surprised.

"I am not sure about all of this but I can tell that you have changed," said her father. "We shall talk about this more tomorrow when the queen comes. But this much I do know, you have been a sweet and kind girl and have helped the queen and the king. I am proud of you." He kissed Liraz on her cheek.

"Yes, you have been given many great gifts this day," said her mother. "But for now, it is time for you to get some sleep." She guided Liraz to her sleeping mat and tucked the blanket around her. "We are proud of you, Liraz. And we love you," she said as she kissed her daughter good night.

And it came to pass that Liraz knew that someday her parents would believe in the Lord as she did. She was glad she had been kind to the queen and had been very blessed because of it.

LEARNING ACTIVITY: KINDNESS

* At family home evening, bake treats with your family. Put them on a plate with big hearts cut out of paper to put on top. Then secretly deliver them to one of your neighbors. Ring their doorbell and run away and hide! Don't let them catch you! You can do this for more than one family. Have fun being the Secret Angel!

* Read in Alma 20 to find out more about Ammon's mission and what happens to him next.

DID YOU KNOW?

* The name Liraz means "I have a secret."

* There are over 56,000 LDS missionaries like Ammon serving throughout the world. The missionaries are serving in about 150 countries. At the Missionary Training Center in Provo, Utah, they teach over 50 different languages! Think of what it is like to hear all those languages being spoken at once when they all eat lunch in the cafeteria!

Twelve

MATAN, THE BRAVE DRUMMER

And it came to pass Matan, son of Jared and Hallel, beat on his drum loudly. "Boom, boom, boom!" went the drum.

"Matan! Go play that drum outside!" called his mother. Matan scooted outside into the bright sunshine. He squinted his eyes.

Matan was a chubby boy with big cheeks and big hands. He had dark skin and dark straight hair that looked even darker next to his yellow shirt. Matan always had a smile on his face and his eyes crinkled so that you could hardly see them. He was the youngest of a large family. His brother was the oldest and was married with a family of his own. Then there were seven sisters. And then came Matan. His name meant "gift." His father had named him because he was happy to finally have another boy in the family!

Matan's family were Lamanites. They lived in the land of Midian.

His father Jared had given Matan the drum for his birthday, and Matan loved it dearly. It was tan on top and bottom. His father had spent many nights teaching Matan the drum beats that helped the villages "talk" to one another.

Jared was responsible for all the drummers in the land. There was a big drum in the big tower, and Jared would go up to signal the people and the other drummers in other villages when they needed to gather or when there was danger. Each set of drumbeats meant something different, and Matan was learning them quickly.

Boom, boom, boom! Matan marched around his house. *Boom, boom, boom!*

His mother stepped out from the house. "Matan, I'm tired and I want to take a nap. Can you play your drum out in the fields? I'm sure the sheep would love to hear it."

Matan laughed and ran down the path to the edge of the town. He knew that when he played his drum, the sheep would run away. But it was sure fun!

He saw several men walking ahead of him on the road, and he ran to catch up with them.

"And who is this fine young man with the big drum?" asked one of the men. Matan recognized him as a Nephite.

"I am Matan, son of the drummer," he answered.

"That drum is almost as big as you are!" said the other Nephite man.

Matan smiled a big smile. "Yes, but when I grow bigger, my drum will be smaller and smaller!" All the men laughed.

"Where are you going?" asked Matan.

"My name is Ammon, and these are my brothers," replied the first Nephite. "We are going to meet with your king and his brother."

Matan's eyes grew big. He had heard from his parents about Ammon and his brothers. They were Nephite missionaries who had been teaching the people about the gospel of Jesus Christ and many of his family had joined the church. Matan was still too young to be baptized, but he believed all the things his parents had talked about.

"My parents are happy you have come to teach our people," said Matan. Ammon and his brothers smiled.

"So, you and your family are Anti-Nephi-Lehies?"

Ammon said. This was the new name of the Lamanites who had joined the church.

"Yes," answered Matan proudly.

"Well, that is a great thing," said Ammon as he patted Matan on both shoulders. "We shall tell your king that there is a great young drummer who believes." With that, Ammon and his brothers hurried up the road, and Matan walked into the fields to go scare the sheep.

Later that night, the family was gathered for dinner.

"The king has called a meeting of the Anti-Nephi-Lehi people tomorrow," said Jared. "I must go send the signal to all the villages. Matan, would you come help me?" The boy nodded happily. That night he and his father drummed out the message from the tower.

The next day many, many people gathered outside the village. The king spoke in a loud voice. "My people. Thanks be to my God that he hath granted unto us that we might repent of these things and also that he hath forgiven us of those our many sins and murders which we have committed. Let us now bury all our swords and never use them again."

Matan could see that a great big hole had been dug in one of the fields. All the people who had joined the church brought all their swords and weapons and threw them into the big pit. Then several strong men shoveled the dirt and filled up the hole.

"Let us promise our God that rather than fight our brothers, we will give up our own lives. We will be true to our God," said the king. All the people agreed with the king.

As Matan and his family walked home, Matan was worried. He had heard his parents talking and saying that the other Lamanites who had not joined the church were very angry and wanted to kill the Anti-Nephi-Lehi people. Matan's mother walked up beside him.

"Do not worry, little one," she said. "We believe in the Lord and whatever happens is His will. Just be brave and believe in Him." Matan felt better.

Several weeks later, Matan was playing in front of his house when he heard the drum. "Boom-de-dah-boom. BOOM!" Matan ran into the house. "Mother! Mother!" he called. "It is the war drum." Hallel ran to the door. "Are you sure?" she asked. Matan stood next to her as his sisters gathered behind him. "Yes. Father taught it to me last week. That means the Lamanites are coming to attack!"

Soon the streets were filled with men walking quickly to the edge of the village. They had no weapons but were walking calmly forward. Women and children stood in their doorways, crying quietly.

Hallel gathered her daughters and her son to the back of the house. "Children, we must pray. Let us pray for our men." The family gathered and began to pray.

The day passed slowly, and finally Jared, their father, came in quietly. Hallel ran to him. "What has happened?" she cried.

Jared slowly sat in a chair beside the fire. He rubbed his face with his hands.

"The Lamanites came and attacked." The whole family gasped.

"Our men bravely stood in the field. Then they kneeled in prayer together. The Lamanites began to attack them. But after a time, they stopped. They could see that our men were not fighting back and they felt bad. Thousands of the Lamanites have now thrown down their weapons and have joined our people."

"What?" asked Hallel in surprise.

"Yes, the Lamanite warriors felt terrible. Now they have gathered in the village and our men are teaching them the gospel," replied Jared. "Now, Matan, I need you to help me."

Matan looked up at his father.

"There are still Lamanites in the fields around us who

are still very angry. I must get a message to the king. But if I go, they will be suspicious. I need you to take your drum and get close to the next village. I will give you a message to beat out, and they will send it to the king. Will you do that?" asked his father.

Matan gulped. His mother stood in front of him. "He is too young!" she exclaimed.

"He is a brave boy," answered his father. "And he knows the beats. We must get this message to the king."

Hallel nodded her head. Both parents hugged Matan, and his father gave him a paper with the beats written on it. Matan grabbed his drum and went out the door.

He quickly made his way out of the village and down the road. After a time, three Lamanite warriors stood in his way. Their faces had red paint on them, and they held spears and swords. "What have we here?" said one Lamanite with three white feathers on a strap around his forehead. Matan felt afraid. But then he remembered that his father had said he was a brave boy. He stood up straight.

"Are you real Lamanite warriors?" asked Matan.

The men stood strongly. "Yes, we are," answered the first man.

"I'm learning to be a big drummer," said Matan. "Do you want me to show you how?"

The three Lamanites laughed. "Sure, let's hear your big drum," said one of the men.

Matan beat his drum loudly. He had been studying the paper and remembered all the beats. He beat his drum loudly over and over again. The men clapped in time with the drum.

"Well, that was very good," said the first Lamanite. "But it is time for all young drummers to get home."

Matan nodded his head and ran off toward his village. He laughed because he had been able to deliver the drum beat message to the next village, and the Lamanite warriors didn't even know.

And it came to pass that Matan was proud that he had been able to be brave. He knew that he had helped his people. He wanted to be like the men who believed in God and were very brave in front of the Lamanite army. He promised himself that he would always stand up for what he believed in.

- Have a family home evening and talk about times when members of your family were brave. Have your parents share with you the stories from Church history when early members of the Church and the pioneers were brave. There are many stories of bravery that you will enjoy hearing.

- You might enjoy making your own drum as an activity for family home evening. You can use a big can or oatmeal box and put a pie tin, waxed paper, or leather over the ends. Have fun!

- Read in Alma 27 to find out how the Anti-Nephi-Lehi people escape and join the Nephites.

DID YOU KNOW?

- The name *Matan* means "gift."

- Drums in Book of Mormon times were made of wood. Some were round like a wooden log that was empty in the middle with animal skins stretched over the ends. Some were shaped like a rectangle. They were called "teponatzle." They had parts of the top cut out and the drummer would hit these parts with a mallet (like a hammer) to make different sounds.

Thirteen

NAAMA IS HUMBLE

And it came to pvass Naama, daughter of Zoram and Timna, spread out her skirt so that everyone could see the beautiful purple flowers that were sewn along the edge. She folded her hands in her lap so that her many bracelets with their beautiful gems of green and red would catch the light just right.

Surely she was the most beautiful girl at synagogue (church) that day. Her father Zoram was very rich and she was able to buy anything she wanted. Her skirt had cost a great deal because purple thread was so difficult to find. Her white blouse set off her dark long curls. She had silver strands tied to her headband that made her hair look especially lovely. She just knew that everyone was looking at her and she hoped they felt jealous.

Naama's father, Zoram, was the leader of the people who called themselves Zoramites. They lived in Antionum which was on the seashore. Her father had many ships and had a big fishing business and trading business so he made lots of money. The Zoramites had left Zarahemla and the Nephites because they didn't like their government, and they didn't want to belong to their church.

Naama looked around the synagogue. She could see Alma, the high priest of the Nephites, and his sons standing in the back. Her father had said bad things about them and didn't want them there. She could tell that Alma was not happy.

Soon it was Naama's turn. The Zoramites had a strange way of having church. Each person would take a turn climbing up to a very high standing place called the Rameumptom. They would go one at a time. And now it was Naama's turn.

She climbed up the steps very high. Standing at the top, she looked up to the sky and said, "Holy, holy God." She was really thinking that she must look beautiful up there high above everybody else and hoped that her friends were noticing her beautiful skirt and jewelry.

"We believe that thou has separated us from our brethren. And thou has elected us that we shall be saved." Naama liked that part. It was fun to think that she and her people were so important and more important than anybody else. She kept saying the words of the prayer that she had been taught.

But just as she was finishing, she looked down. She could see outside the synagogue toward the center of the city. There, just beside a building, she could see her friend Ruth. She was surprised. She had not seen Ruth in a few months. Her friend looked very sad. Naama made her way carefully down the steps of the Rameumptom.

The meeting was over as everyone had had a turn to say their loud prayer and they were all going back to their homes. She could hear loud voices. Alma and his sons were talking to her father and other leaders of the city.

"This isn't a church," said Alma. "You aren't worshipping God. You are just bragging."

"Just because we don't worship the same way you do . . ." began Zoram.

"No, you know this is wrong. Christ never taught us to be cruel to other people and to think we are better than them. Christ wants all of us to be saved. He loves all people," said Alma.

"Well, we don't believe that. We believe that we are the only ones to be saved," argued Zoram.

"You need to repent," said Shiblon, Alma's son. "You have been taught the truth and have twisted it to something false. You need to study your scriptures and be humble and repent."

"We have nothing to be humble about," said Zoram, and he pushed his way past the men. Naama and her mother and brothers followed behind.

"Mother," said Naama when they were in the street. "I saw my friend Ruth. Why doesn't she come to synagogue anymore?"

"Her father got sick and couldn't work. Your father had to take his job away from him and give it to someone else. I have heard that they had many bills to pay and have lost everything. Ruth is poor now, and we don't let poor people come to the synagogue," said her mother.

"Why not?" said Naama.

"That's just the way it is. Your father has decided it," said her mother.

Naama was very sad. She had really liked her friend Ruth.

The next day Naama decided to go look for her friend. She went to her house and knocked on the door, asking for Ruth. "They don't live here anymore," said the woman. "They have moved to the south edge of town."

Naama decided to go find her. She walked for a long time and finally came to a dark and crowded street. She stopped at a small doorway, "Hello?" she called. Her friend Ruth came to the door.

"Naama! What are you doing here?" said Ruth.

"I heard about what happened to your family and wanted to say how sorry I am," said Naama.

"Sorry? Your father did this to us. My father worked for him for many years. He was getting better but your father would not wait. We have lost everything!" said Ruth as she began to cry.

Naama felt very bad. "How can I help you?"

"You cannot help," said Ruth. "You just go with your fancy clothes and your expensive jewels and live in your big house. You just go on pretending that those of us who are poor are not important." And she shut the door.

Naama stood there in shock. She made her way back home and thought about what Ruth had said. She did not feel good about what her father had been teaching her. She didn't believe that God only loved the rich and not the poor. She felt that it was important to help others. And she realized that she had been very selfish.

The next day Naama heard some women talking who said that Alma, the prophet, was preaching on the hill Onidah, which was outside of town. She decided to go listen.

As she sat on the side of the hill listening to Alma and Amulek preach, a large group of poor people came to Alma.

"What shall we do?" one of them asked. "We are poor and they won't let us in the synagogue to pray and worship."

"You don't need to worship God only in church and only once a week," said Alma. "It is good that this has happened to you because now you are humble. Now you will listen to our message and believe in God. He that truly humbleth himself, and repenteth of his sins, and endureth to the end, the same shall be blessed."

Naama thought about this. And she thought about what Ruth had said to her. She had not been humble. She had been really proud of being rich and having expensive things. She had not been kind to others. She did believe in Christ and knew the things that Alma said were true.

As she was thinking, someone sat down beside her. "Ruth!" she said. "What are you doing here?"

Ruth looked toward the sea. "I came to say I was sorry. I was not very nice to you. It's not your fault that my father lost his job," she said.

Naama patted her hand. "Oh no. I am the one who is sorry. I never really believed the things my father and the others were teaching. I have been selfish and greedy. I am so sorry that I wasn't a true friend to you. I have much to change. Will you forgive me?"

The two friends hugged each other.

And it came to pass that Naama felt very humbled. She knew that she had things she needed to change in her life. She also had learned that she was no better than anybody else. She was humble enough to believe in Christ and to repent and to love others like she knew she should.

LEARNING ACTIVITY: HUMILITY

- ☀ Talk with your mother or father about things in your life you can do better. Maybe you can be kinder to your brother or sister or maybe you can be more cheerful. Pick one thing you want to work on and set a goal to work on it all week. Write down your goal or draw a picture to put up in your room to remind you.

- ☀ Read in Alma 36 where Alma writes letters to his sons.

DID YOU KNOW?

- ☀ The name *Naama* means "pleasant."

- ☀ In Book of Mormon times, the color purple was made from certain kinds of shellfish. Cloth was made with stripes, diagonal patterns, or diamonds woven in as designs. The weavers could even make complicated designs like animals or flowers. Some designs were sewn on the fabric with thread and needles.

Fourteen

ODED LOVES LIBERTY

And it came to pass Oded, grandson of Gershon, fell flat on his face. "Ha-ha!" laughed the big boy. "Made you fall!"

Oded started to get up when all of a sudden, he felt like he was flying. Then he realized that a big man was lifting him up high onto his shoulders.

"And who dares to treat this fine warrior this way?" boomed the man at the mean boy.

"Warrior? That kid's no warrior. He can't even walk right!" laughed the boy.

"This boy is going to be a great warrior, and he shall fight by my side," said the big man. "Would you like us to start now and show you?" He leaned toward the mean boy. The boy looked scared and ran off. Then the big man lowered Oded to the ground.

"And who are you, my muddy friend?" he asked. Oded was covered in mud from falling.

"I am Oded, grandson of Gershon," he answered quietly.

"Gershon! Why he was a great warrior! How is the old man doing?" said the big man as he sat down beside Oded.

"My grandfather is doing well," he said. "How do you know my grandfather?"

"I fought with him in several battles. He taught me much," the man replied.

"I have been digging clams to take home to him for dinner," said Oded.

"Well, I believe that I shall join you for dinner," said the big man. And with that he helped Oded gather all the clams in the basket and swung him back up to his shoulders. Oded balanced the basket on the big man's head.

Soon they were at Oded's home. "Gershon, I have something for you," called the big man. An older man came to the doorway and, seeing the big man, ran to him and gave him a big bear hug. Oded almost dropped his basket but was able to keep it perched on the big man's head.

"Moroni! How wonderful to see you!" said Oded's grandfather. Oded swung his head down to look at the big man.

"You're Captain Moroni?" he said with his eyes opened big and wide.

"Yes, I am," replied the big man, and he swung Oded and his basket down to the ground.

"Are you really in charge of all the Nephite armies?" asked Oded.

"Yes, he is," answered his grandfather. "Now let the man sit down and don't pester him." Captain Moroni and Gershon sat at the table. Oded sat down in a small chair next to them.

Oded was a skinny boy with dark reddish-brown hair and green eyes. He wore a brown robe with a red sash. He lived with his grandfather and his older sister. His father had been killed in a war, and his mother had died from the river fever. He missed his mother and father, but he did love his grandfather dearly.

Oded stood and limped over to the fire to move the

pot with boiling water. Captain Moroni looked at Gershon with his eyebrows raised.

"He was injured when he was a little boy," explained Gershon quietly. "His leg never healed right and he walks with a limp. Poor child—the other children make fun of him because of it."

"Well, we'll see what we can do about that," said Moroni. "So, my old friend, let's talk of our battles! I remember you making me practice throwing my spear at a log for hours on end." Both men laughed.

They all had a good dinner of clams and bread. They sat by the fire. "I am worried about the government," said Captain Moroni. "Amalickiah has been getting the lower judges to support him. He wants to take over as king of the land."

"That would be terrible," said Gershon. "They would take away all of our freedoms. What shall we do?"

"I am not sure, but I have to do something," answered Moroni. "I'm going to pray about it, and I'm sure the Lord will help. But now, I must be going. Thank you, Oded, for those delicious clams. It was good to meet a fine young warrior like yourself." Oded's face turned red, and he looked at his feet.

Gershon smiled. "Take care of yourself, my friend."

Several days later, Oded was walking through the center of the city. He saw Captain Moroni arguing with several men. "You cannot take our freedoms away!" Moroni shouted. "With the help of the Lord, we will stop you!" Captain Moroni turned and stomped away from the men. As he was leaving, he saw Oded.

"Oded!" he called quietly. "It is time. Will you help me?"

"Y-y-yes," stammered Oded.

"Then come with me," said Captain Moroni. They went quickly to Captain Moroni's home.

Oded watched as Captain Moroni took his light tan coat and tore off a big piece of fabric. He took a piece of coal and wrote on it, "In memory of our God, our religion, and freedom, and our peace, our wives, and our children." He tied the fabric to a long pole.

"Help me, Oded," he said. "I'm going to put on my armor."

Oded helped Captain Moroni put on his head-plate, his breastplate, and his armor. He helped Captain Moroni tie each piece on tightly.

"Now, Oded, we must pray." Captain Moroni knelt down and Oded followed. He listened as Captain Moroni prayed with all his heart to the Lord to bless the people that they would choose freedom. After a long time, he finished.

"I am going to hold up this pole very high so the people can read my message," said Captain Moroni. "I would like you to carry my big shield and walk behind me. Will you be my shield bearer, Oded?"

Oded gasped. It was a great honor to be a shield bearer. It meant that he would help protect Captain Moroni.

"But I'm just a boy, and I walk with a limp!" said Oded.

"Today, you are a young warrior helping me fight for freedom. I know you can do it," said Captain Moroni, resting his hand on Oded's shoulder. His hand with the armor on it felt heavy on Oded's shoulder.

"Yes, sir," said Oded, standing straight and tall.

The Captain and his young shield bearer walked out into the sunshine. Captain Moroni walked slowly and strongly so that Oded had no trouble keeping up while he carried the big shield.

They walked to the center of town and climbed the steps of the government building.

Captain Moroni waved his flag back and forth and shouted with a loud voice, "My people! Hear me!" People began to gather in the center of town and soon a large crowd had gathered.

"Behold, whoever will fight for freedom, let them come forward! Whoever will promise the Lord their God that they will protect their rights and their freedom of religion, come join us!" shouted Moroni. Soon people came running from all over the city with their armor on. They ripped their coats as a sign that they would make this promise to the Lord.

But there were some people in the crowd that argued with Captain Moroni. "Amalickiah should be king! We won't have you telling us what to do!"

As all of this was happening, Oded was standing off to the side of Captain Moroni. He didn't realize that a group of boys had gathered until suddenly they began to throw rocks at him.

"What!" he cried. He ducked down behind Moroni's big shield. The rocks hit the shield. Ping! Ping! A few hit Oded on the shoulder and one barely missed his head. He was scared and knew that Captain Moroni was busy and couldn't help him. But after a while, he got angry. Then he got angry with himself. Finally, he stood up and faced the group of boys and recognized the big mean boy who had tripped him days earlier.

"Stop what you are doing this instant!" he shouted to the boys. The boys were so surprised they stopped. "I am here as shield bearer to Captain Moroni, who is commander of all our armies. We are here to fight for freedom. You are silly boys. It is time for you to be men! Will you fight against our freedoms?"

At that, several boys paused to think and then dropped their rocks and walked away. Soon, just the big mean boy was left. He looked around and realized he was alone.

"What is your choice?" called Oded to the boy. "I choose to stand for freedom this day. What do you choose?"

The boy looked at Oded and looked at Captain Moroni. Then he turned and walked away.

Oded did not realize that Captain Moroni had come to stand behind him.

"See, I knew that you had the heart of a great warrior," said Captain Moroni, "just like your father and your grandfather." Oded smiled. "You shall stand behind me as we call the people to support freedom."

Oded stood tall and held the shield up high.

And it came to pass that Oded knew that it was important to protect the freedom of the land. He knew that he could be brave and strong and do what was right. And he was proud to be helping in the battle for freedom because Oded loved liberty.

LEARNING ACTIVITY: PATRIOTISM

※ Ask your mother or father to read to you stories of George Washington, Thomas Jefferson, Benjamin Franklin, Abraham Lincoln, and other great men and women who helped make our country free. Perhaps you have stories of your grandfathers who fought in a war that they could share with you.

※ For family home evening, have your family write letters to someone serving in the military.

※ Read in Alma 46–47 to find out what else Captain Moroni does. He was a great leader in his fight to protect the freedom of the people.

DID YOU KNOW?

※ The name *Oded* means "to encourage." Captain Moroni really encouraged Oded, didn't he?

※ Warriors in Book of Mormon times made their shields out of the hides of animals. Some were long and flexible and some were smaller, round, and rigid. The shields helped to protect them from the arrows and the spears of the armies that were attacking them.

※ The armies would follow what was called a "battle standard." It was made of tall spears with large square or round shields attached to the tops of the spears. These shields had decorations painted on and attached to them. They were usually edged with bright feathers. This helped the armies see where their leaders were and where they were supposed to go in the battle.

Fifteen

PELIA HAS FAITH

And it came to pass that Pelia, daughter of Amir and Rina, gathered her skirts in both hands and jumped down off the ladder. Her dark golden braids from either side of her head were tied with a leather strap at the bottom and they bounced over her head as she landed softly in the dirt.

"Hey, what are you doing there?" yelled a Lamanite guard.

"Oh, I was just looking at the sunset," said Pelia, and she skipped past the guard quickly and went down the path.

"Well, stay off of the ladders!" he yelled at her back. Pelia giggled as she broke out in a run.

Pelia lived with her mother, father, and two older brothers in the city of Manti near the seashore. She was small but very strong and tried hard to keep up with her brothers. Her father was off fighting in the war against the Lamanites with Captain Moroni. Pelia frowned as she thought about her father. He had been gone a long time, and she wondered if he was safe. She also wondered if he knew that the Lamanites had taken over their city of Manti.

Pelia glared at the Lamanite soldiers that were standing here and there in the streets. Her friends were afraid of the soldiers, but Pelia was mostly angry. How dare they come and take over her city! She would do everything she could to fight against them.

But Pelia was just a young girl. What could she do? The Lamanite army had been in her city for a very long time. They had already killed many of the people of her city. Where were the Nephite armies? Would they ever come and save her and her city?

Soon she arrived at the door of her home. She went in and saw her mother setting food on the table. Her mother, Rina, had dark golden hair like her daughter, but streaks of gray were here and there. Pelia went to her mother and kissed her on the cheek.

"Where have you been?" exclaimed her mother in surprise. "I've been worried about you!"

"I'm sorry, Mother," answered Pelia. "I was on the ladders looking to see if the Nephite armies had come yet."

"It's been over a year," said her brother as he grabbed a piece of bread. "I don't think they are going to come."

"Oh, Ezra, don't say that. We must have faith in the Lord and He will help us," said their mother.

"But we've been praying and praying," said Pelia. "When will our prayers be answered? Is God really listening to us?"

"He always listens to us," said her mother. "But He answers our prayers when it is His time, not ours. Our job is to have great faith that He knows what is best for us."

"I do have faith in Him," said Pelia. "I just know that He will help us. Every day I pray for a miracle."

"Good girl," smiled her mother. "You keep that up and we'll have a miracle." The family sat to eat dinner.

The next day Pelia was walking through the city when she saw a Lamanite young man walking by. He stood by the ladder that Pelia had climbed the day before. He pushed on the rungs of the ladder.

"It's strong enough to hold you," said Pelia.

"And how do you know that?" asked the young Lamanite.

Pelia's face turned red, and she looked at her feet. "I take it you've climbed this ladder a time or two," he said, laughing. Pelia didn't say a word.

"Tell me . . ." said the young man. "Where is your father?" Pelia looked up suddenly.

"He is fighting with the Nephite army," she said.

"Ah, that is good," said the young man quietly. Pelia stared at him. "If I tell you something, will you keep quiet about it?" he said.

"I do not keep secrets from my mother," answered Pelia.

"Oh no," said the young man. "I mean don't say anything to the Lamanite soldiers."

Pelia spit on the ground. "I never say *anything* to the soldiers. But aren't you one of them?"

The young man laughed. "Oh no. I certainly am not," he said. "I'm serving with the Nephite army under Helaman. I am of the people of Ammon."

Pelia gasped. "So you are helping us?" she asked.

"Of course," said the young Lamanite. "My name is Oren. I am here as a spy for the Nephite army. We are planning to free your city soon. But you must not say anything to the soldiers."

"Don't worry," said Pelia. "But I thought the people of Ammon wouldn't fight."

"That is true. My parents took a covenant to never take up weapons. But there are two thousand of us who are their sons, and we never made such a promise. We are young warriors here serving to help free our people, and Helaman is our leader. But now I think I could use your help," he explained.

"What can I do?" answered Pelia.

"Tell me about the ladders," said Oren. So Pelia showed Oren all the ladders that the soldiers used to guard the city. Throughout the city, the ladders were leaned against the walls of the city to help the soldiers look over the walls to see if anyone was coming to the city.

Then Oren went to Pelia's home and told her family about the plan to free the city of Manti. "We are going to get the Lamanite army to leave the city and come after us. Then we will send a small group of soldiers from our Nephite army to come back and attack the guards left in the city. Then we will come and your city will be free. But we need your help."

"How can we help you?" asked Rina, Pelia's mother.

"Can you get your friends to help, Pelia?" asked Oren. "It would really help if there weren't any ladders on the north wall. Then the Lamanites won't see our small army coming. The guards won't be watching young children. Can you hide the ladders or move them?"

Pelia laughed. "Oh, yes. We can do that!"

So late in the night, Oren slipped quietly out of the city and went back to report to Helaman. Pelia's family gathered to pray for Oren and the Nephite armies. "I'm praying for that miracle, and I'm going to have lots of faith!" said Pelia.

"Well then, you had better be the one to say the family prayer tonight," answered her mother, and the family knelt together.

Early the next day, Pelia gathered her friends and told them of the plan. All morning long, she and her friends quietly walked around and moved the ladders when the guards weren't looking. Pelia hid one behind a stack of sticks. Her friend Leila laid one down and covered it with bundles of food. Tamara was brave and took two different ladders and untied all the rungs so that they were just a pile of sticks. By the end of the morning, there were no ladders left on the north wall.

As the sun rose high in the sky, a shout went up from the east side of the city. "A small Nephite army is moving."

Pelia and her family watched as the leader of the Lamanite army gathered all of his soldiers together. They all seemed very excited. "We shall destroy this small army easily!" shouted their leader. "Our spies tell us that they are just young men and boys."

Pelia held her breath. She was worried for Oren and his friends and said a quick prayer that Heavenly Father would keep them safe.

Then the Lamanite army marched swiftly out of the city gate. A small group of Lamanite guards were left behind. They stood by the gate with their weapons ready.

After several hours had passed, there was shouting and pounding on the gate.

"What is it?" cried one of the guards.

"It is a Nephite army!" yelled another.

"Why didn't we see them coming?" said the first guard.

"We didn't see them from the walls," said the second guard.

Pelia watched from a doorway and stood in the shadows. She giggled quietly as she realized their plan had worked. The Nephite army had been able to sneak up to the city from the north and the guards had not seen them!

Soon the gate doors swung open as a group of Nephite soldiers burst through. They fought with the Lamanite guards and were able to capture them quickly. Soon more Nephite soldiers and a group of the Lamanite stripling warriors came through and took up positions inside the city.

"Watch the north and west walls!" called their leader. Pelia stepped out of the doorway.

"Sir!" she called. "We have hidden the ladders on the north. We will get them for you."

"Ah, so you are the little one who has helped us rescue your city," said the Nephite commander.

"Yes, sir," answered Pelia.

"Well, your city is now safe, and we thank you and your friends for your help," said the man.

"We thank the Lord," said Pelia. "We prayed for a miracle, and you are here. You are an answer to our prayers."

The Nephite leader patted her on the head. "Yes, the Lord has helped us all," he said.

Just then, Oren came forward and stood by Pelia.

"Well, Pelia. You are free!" he said.

"Yes," said Pelia. "Thank you to you and your warriors."

"Our prayers and our faith in the Lord have protected us all," said Oren. "Our mothers told us that if we would have faith, we would be protected. And we have been."

"My mother told me to have faith as well," said Pelia.

And it came to pass that Pelia knew her faith in the Lord had been rewarded. A miracle had happened and they were safe and free. She knew that her faith would grow stronger and stronger and that someday when she was a mother, she would teach her children to have faith in the Lord as well.

LEARNING ACTIVITY: FAITH

- ✺ Ask your mother or father to share with you stories from your family and your ancestors of faith. Have them share with you how they first received a testimony of the Lord.

- ✺ Read in Alma 53–58 to find out more about the adventures of Helaman and the 2,000 stripling warriors.

DID YOU KNOW?

- ✺ The name Pelia means "miracle."

- ✺ The cities in the Book of Mormon times were surrounded by large walls to keep the people safe. There were large gates in the walls to let the people come and go. They lived inside the city walls and would go out during the day to tend to their crops and their animals. During battles, armies would use tall ladders to see over the walls to protect their city.

Sixteen

RACHEL KEEPS THE SABBATH DAY HOLY

And it came to pass that Rachel, daughter of Omni and Dena, pounded the pile of clay with her fist. Then she used her thumb and fingers to push a hole into the middle of the wet clay and worked with it until she had made a small pot.

Rachel was a solid girl with strong arms and a pleasant face. Her brown hair was braided and tied in a bun on the back of her head but short curls fell forward into her face. She wore a black skirt and golden blouse with a dusty brown apron. She sat on a small stool in her parents' shop and worked the clay carefully.

"Mad at someone?" asked her father, Omni. He sat at the large potter's wheel and pumped the foot pedal to make the wheel turn. He had a tall pot in the middle that he was working on as it spun around and around.

Rachel looked up at him. "Why do you ask that?" she asked.

"Well, you've been pounding that clay pretty hard!" Her father laughed.

"It's fun to pound!" said Rachel's little brother, who was busily pounding the floor with a wood mallet.

"I'm just in a hurry to get this done," said Rachel as she worked even faster.

Rachel's parents had a pottery shop near the center of town. Her family had left the city of Zarahemla with many others and had traveled far to the land northward. They lived in a cement house that her father had built. Her parents had set up their pottery shop and were doing very well selling their pots and lamps. Her father made the large pots, and her mother, a great artist, would paint the pots in bright colors with beautiful flowers, animals, and designs. Their business was very successful. Their pots were very popular, and they even were able to ship them down to Zarahemla and other cities in the south to be sold.

Rachel liked living in the land northward. The clay here near the river and the hills was very red. She liked to help her father and mother dig up the clay and clean it to use in making the lamps and pots. Rachel thought it was funny that their hands stayed kind of orange most of the time no matter how much they washed. But her mother, Dena, did not like it at all and worked hard to try to get their clothes and their hands white and clean. She was always calling to Rachel's little brother to stay out of the dirt. But it didn't help. Rachel's little brother loved the red dirt.

"Rachel, don't forget you need to deliver those five lamps to the storekeeper before the Sabbath," said her mother.

"I know, I know," said Rachel. But as the afternoon passed, Rachel found herself doing one thing or another. Then there was a knock at the door. She went to the door, wiping her hands on her apron.

"Rachel! Come play with us!" It was her friend Miriam. Rachel looked around the shop. Her mother and father were in the house and only her older sister was there sweeping. She saw the five small lamps lined up by her stool. Well, she would just hurry and go play for a short while, she thought.

She called to her sister to tell her she was going with her friends to play and ran out the door.

Rachel and her friends ran through the streets of the city playing hide and seek. The new cement houses had large doorways and were perfect to hide in. "I'm going to count to fifty," said Jorash, the baker's son. He began to count slowly. Rachel grabbed Miriam. "I've got a great hiding place—come on!" The two girls ran down the street. Soon they stood at a tall ladder. "Climb up here!" said Rachel.

"But where are we?" asked Miriam.

"It's the back of Shayna's house," said Rachel, pushing her friend up the ladder. Up they climbed to the roof of the house.

The cement houses were often hot by the end of the day and many of the families had built a flat area on the tops of their houses with a low wall around it. They would climb up in the evenings and sit there to watch the sunset and to cool off and be together. Rachel and Miriam stood on the top and peeked over the wall.

"He'll never find us here!" said Miriam, and the two girls giggled as they hid behind the low wall. Soon they couldn't stop giggling and laughing. They tried covering their mouths, but they kept giggling.

"Aha!" said Jorash as he stood on the top of the ladder. "I've found you!"

"How could you find us?" said Miriam with her hands on her hips.

"The whole city could hear you two up here laughing," said Jorash. "Now it's your turn to count!" The girls followed him down the ladder to gather with the rest of the children.

After a long time, Rachel realized that it was getting dark. She said good-bye to her friends and ran home. She ran into her house, and her mother stood lighting the lamps with her shawl over her head.

"Good Sabbath," said her mother.

"Good Sabbath to you," replied Rachel.

"Help me light the lamps," said her mother, and Rachel helped her mother light the oil lamps they had in their home. Each one was beautiful and different.

"Oh!" said Rachel. "I forgot to deliver those lamps to the storekeeper! I should go."

"But it is the Sabbath," answered her mother. "It is not time to work. We must keep the Sabbath day holy."

"But I heard the storekeeper tell you that they had to be delivered today or he would not pay," said Rachel.

"Yes, he did," said her mother. "You are old enough to decide. We have taught you to keep the Sabbath day holy. Now you must choose what you are going to do."

Rachel walked into the pottery shop next to their house. She looked at the five lamps next to her stool. If she didn't deliver them, the storekeeper might not pay for them. She knew that it would not be good to lose the money. But if she did deliver them, that would be working and that would also be breaking the Sabbath. Rachel stared at the lamps for a time. Then she turned and went back into her home.

The next day, the family gathered and walked to church. Rachel sat next to her mother and older sister.

Helaman, the leader of the Nephites, had traveled to their city to meet with the people. He stood to speak.

"My brothers and sisters, I am happy to be here among you this day. You have built a fine city with these many cement houses and shops, and I am proud of you. I bring you good news from Zarahemla. We have suffered much from Gadianton and his band of robbers. Some of you have suffered at the hands of these robbers. I am happy to report that they have fled into the wilderness, and the city is once again safe and the people are well."

There were murmurs and whispering as the people in church heard the good news.

"Now I would like to speak to you today about an important thing. I will be speaking about keeping the Sabbath day holy. Let's read from the scriptures." Helaman turned to the scroll next to him and unrolled it to read. "Remember the sabbath day, to keep it holy. Six days shalt thou labor, and do all thy work. But the seventh day is the sabbath of the Lord thy God: in it thou shalt not do any work, thou, nor thy son, nor thy daughter, thy manservant, nor thy maidservant, nor thy cattle, nor thy stranger that is within thy gates. For in six days the Lord made heaven and earth, the sea, and all that in them is, and rested the seventh day: wherefore the Lord blessed the sabbath day, and hallowed it."

Rachel's head popped up. She looked sideways at her mother and her mother smiled.

And it came to pass that Rachel knew that she had made the right choice to keep the Sabbath day holy. She knew that it was an important day to worship the Lord.

LEARNING ACTIVITY: KEEP SABBATH DAY HOLY

☀ Have your family help you get a jar or small container. Then write down on small papers, or draw pictures, of things you can do on the Sabbath day. You can include things like "Sing Primary songs," "Write or draw in my journal," "Read the *Friend* magazine," "Watch a Church video," or other things you can think of. On the next Sunday, pull out one or more of the papers and do what is on the paper.

☀ Read in Helaman 2–3 to find out about the people who moved to the land northward. Why did they build their houses out of cement?

DID YOU KNOW?

☀ The name Rachel means "purity."

☀ There are many cities made of stone and cement in the southern parts of the United States and Central and South America that still stand. Some of these were built on the sides of cliffs to protect the people. In the United States, two national parks have these villages—Mesa Verde National Park and Casa Grande National Monument. Have your parents help you go on the Internet, so you can see pictures of them and the other cities in Central and South America made of stone and cement.

Seventeen

SOLOMON IS A PEACEMAKER

And it came to pass that Solomon, brother of Amos, rubbed the wooden spoon with a bundle of leather. The spoon was almost smooth. He had been working on it all morning.

"Don't take all day with that," called his brother. "We have more to finish."

"I'm almost done," said Solomon.

Solomon was a very young Lamanite boy. He still had chubby arms and legs as a young boy would and had short, straight black hair. He wore a simple brown robe that used to be his brother's. He lived in the land of Nephi with his older brother, Amos, and his older sister, Jethra. Their parents had died from a sickness when Solomon was very little. Solomon's brother took over their father's carpentry business. They made all kinds of things from wood, including tables, chairs, tools, and, of course, spoons. Solomon tried to help his brother and sister. He liked to sand and smooth all the things they made. And today he was working on this spoon.

Jethra walked out of the shop. She was tall, with beautiful long dark hair that hung to her waist. She was carrying two chairs. "I'm going to take these chairs over to the wife of the captain."

"They are beautiful!" said Solomon. "You have painted them with pretty colors!"

Jethra laughed. "Yes, they're very colorful. They are a gift from the captain to his wife, and he paid dearly for them."

"They sure look good," said Solomon. And Jethra walked down the street with the two chairs.

Their shop was near the large prison that stood at the end of town. Solomon liked sitting on his little stool outside of the door of their shop so that he could see what was happening in the city. He rubbed his spoon some more.

"Well, Nephi, I wonder if today is the day."

Solomon looked up at the window of the prison where the voice came from. For many days, he had been listening to the two men who were in the prison. They were the Nephite brothers Nephi and Lehi, who some said were prophets. The Lamanite leaders had thrown them into prison.

"What is today?" Solomon called up to the window.

He could barely see the face of one of the men at the window. "Ah, our little carpenter is here working again today," said the man who Solomon recognized as Nephi.

"I'm working on this spoon," said Solomon as he held up the wooden spoon.

"You are a good worker," said Lehi, from the other window.

Nephi and Lehi had been telling Solomon the stories of the scriptures. He loved to hear them tell about Moses parting the Red Sea and about Christ who would come to visit the people. Every day he sat on his stool and talked to the two men.

Just then a group of older children came rushing around the corner. They stood arguing with each other.

"Let's take this son of a Nephite and beat him up!" said one boy with an angry snarl. Solomon recognized the boy whose father was a Nephite and who had come to live in their city for a short time.

"Leave him alone," yelled a tall girl with her hands in fists.

"We can do what we want," yelled another boy. "And you can't stop us!"

The group of children split into two groups, yelling and shouting at each other. Their fists were raised, and one boy stepped forward, ready to fight.

Solomon jumped up from his stool.

"Stop!" he yelled. The children stepped back.

"And who are you?" said the angry boy.

"I am Solomon," he said.

"You're just a baby!" said the tall girl.

"I may be little, but I know it's not good to fight," said Solomon. "Fighting never helps with anything."

The children stood for a moment with their fists ready to fight.

"Aw, the little kid is right," said a big boy with black eyes. "We're friends. Why are we fighting?"

The children lowered their hands and began to talk to one another. They walked off together down the street.

"Well, my little peacemaker," called Lehi from the window. "Well done!"

Solomon smiled. "I just remembered you telling me about Moses trying to get the children of Israel not to fight all the time."

Nephi and Lehi laughed.

Then Solomon saw a large group of hundreds of angry Lamanites and Nephites walk past the street.

"Nephi, Lehi! Lots of angry men are coming, and they're headed to the prison," he called up to the window.

"Do not worry, Solomon," said Nephi. "The Lord is with us."

Solomon watched as hundreds of men went into the prison. He scooted over to the doorway, and no one noticed as he stood just inside. The men were shouting.

"It is time for your death!" yelled the men as they went to Nephi and Lehi's cell, their room in the prison surrounded by iron bars.

Then Solomon looked in to Nephi and Lehi's cell. It was filled with bright light, almost as if Nephi and Lehi were surrounded by fire. The men stood back in fear. They didn't dare touch Nephi and Lehi because they were afraid they would get burned.

"Brothers!" called Nephi and Lehi. "Fear not, for behold it is God that has shown unto you this marvelous thing."

Then the earth shook and the walls of the prison began to shake. Solomon sat down quickly on the ground. He was afraid the building would come down.

A dark cloud filled the prison. No one could see anything. Solomon was feeling very afraid. He heard a still voice above the cloud, "Repent ye, repent ye, and seek no more to destroy my servants." The earth and the prison shook again. Solomon held onto the wall. Then he could see that Nephi and Lehi's faces were shining and they were talking to someone, and he felt less afraid.

Then he heard someone speak. "Who are these Nephites talking to?"

"They are talking to the angels of God," said another man who was a Nephite.

"What can we do to have this dark cloud go away?" said another.

"Repent and pray," said the Nephite man. "You must believe in Christ."

Solomon could hear all the people praying and he too began to pray like Nephi and Lehi had taught him. The people were crying and praying in the dark. Soon the dark cloud went away, and he could see that everyone was surrounded by a bright light with Nephi and Lehi standing in the middle of them. He heard the voice again, "Peace, peace be unto you."

And then a marvelous light came from the top of the prison, and Solomon watched with wonder as he saw angels coming down and talking to all the people in the prison.

Nephi saw Solomon and waved him over. Solomon walked carefully over to him.

"You have seen great things this day," said Nephi. Solomon hugged his friend. "I know you will be faithful to the Lord all your life. Always be a peacemaker, Solomon. Christ brings peace. You must help bring that peace to your people."

And it came to pass that Solomon felt peace in his heart.

He knew that he would carry the love of the Lord to others and work hard his whole life bringing the peace he felt that day to others.

LEARNING ACTIVITY: BEING A PEACEMAKER

☀ Talk to your family about being a peacemaker. Have your family make a chart for the family to work on not having any arguments or fights. For every day you don't fight or argue with members of the family, give yourself a sticker for that day.

☀ Read in Helaman 5 to find out what happened to the people who saw the angels that day. Also read Helaman 10, 11, and 3 Nephi 7 to read about the great miracles performed by Nephi and his brother Lehi.

DID YOU KNOW?

☀ The name Solomon means "peacemaker."

☀ Jesus was raised by Joseph, who was a carpenter. As he grew up, he learned how to make many things from wood including tables, chairs, tools, and other useful things. Carpenters were very important to a village because of the things they could make.

Eighteen

TIRTZA LISTENS TO THE PROPHET

And it came to pass that Tirtza, daughter of Amnon and Uriella, ran through the tall cornstalks as fast as she could with her long reddish-brown braids bouncing behind her.

"Aha!" Her sister Temima popped out between two cornstalks. "Tag! You're it!" She laughed at Tirtza and then turned and ran.

"Oh! I am going to get you!" called Tirtza, and she pulled her light green dress up to her knees and ran back down the row toward her sister.

"Girls! Temima, Tirtza, Tahlia, and Tiva! Come here this minute!"

Four young girls with bobbing braids all ran together to the edge of the cornfield to their father.

Tirtza was the second of four sisters. Their father raised corn and tomatoes in their fields outside of the city of Zarahemla. The girls all helped their father, and it was that time of the season to begin picking the corn.

"Have you girls been working or playing all day?" said their mother, Uriella, as she laid out a blanket and began spreading out the food she had brought for lunch.

"Uh, a little of both!" said Tirzta as she bit into the tomato sandwich. Bits of bread flew out of her mouth as she spoke.

"Watch where you're chewing!" teased her sister Tahlia as she poked her in the ribs. Tirtza smiled a big smile and the tomato she had bitten into covered her teeth.

"I don't know if we're raising daughters or silly animals!" said their mother, smiling at their father. Uriella sat down carefully, rubbing her back. Her big belly stretched her dress.

"Well, let's hope this baby is a calm baby," said Amnon as he patted his wife's belly.

"And a boy!" chimed in all the girls. They were hoping for

a little brother to join their family, although having another sister to play with would be fun too.

"So anything new today in the city?" asked Amnon.

"Well, remember that Lamanite who was preaching in the city?" said Uriella.

"Yes, I believe his name was Samuel," answered Amnon. "What of him?"

"Well, a big group of people threw him out of the city and told him never to return," said Uriella.

"You're kidding," said Tirtza. "Why would they be afraid of a man talking? I was hoping to go listen to him after we were done working."

"Yes, I was too," said Uriella. "But some people get very upset when someone tells them to repent. They don't like being told that they are doing wrong things."

"But many of them *are* doing wrong things!" said Temima.

"Yes, but people who are doing bad things usually don't want to hear about it," answered her mother. "But I liked what I heard of this Samuel the Lamanite. I believe that he was sent from God."

"I felt that way too," said Amnon. "Well, girls, it's time to get back to work. And this time, let's get our work done and then you can play the rest of the day."

The girls jumped up and quickly helped their mother pack up the lunch and blanket and ran to help their father.

The next morning, Tirtza walked toward the city gates. She had stayed behind to help her mother and was heading out of the city to help her family in the fields.

"He's up there!" called a man on her right.

"What is that man doing up there?" called a woman standing by a donkey.

Soon a group of people had gathered. All were looking up to the top of the city wall. Tirtza looked up and gasped. There standing on the top of a wall was a very tall Lamanite man with his black hair blowing in the wind.

"Behold!" called out the man in a loud voice. "I, Samuel, a Lamanite, do speak the words of the Lord!"

Tirtza stood and looked at the man intently. She felt a tingle run through her.

"Repent and have faith on the Lord Jesus Christ!" said Samuel. "Blessed are they who will repent."

"Why is a Lamanite telling us to repent?" grumbled a short man next to Tirza.

"Yeah, who does he think he is?" snarled a tall woman behind her.

Samuel the Lamanite continued to preach to the people and Tirtza listened carefully to every word he said. "Behold I give unto you a sign, for five years more cometh, and behold, then cometh the Son of God to redeem all those who shall believe on his name."

Tirtza was so surprised. Her parents had taught her about Jesus Christ and how the prophets had all said He would come to visit their people. But now Samuel the Lamanite was saying He would be born in five years!

"And behold, this will I give unto you for a sign at the time of his coming, for behold, there shall be great lights in heaven, insomuch that in the night before he cometh there shall be no darkness. . . There shall be one day and a night and a day, as if it were one day and there was no night; and this shall be unto you for a sign; And behold, there shall a new star arise, such an one as ye never have beheld; and this also shall be a sign unto you."

Tirtza felt a warm feeling and knew that Samuel the Lamanite told the truth. She felt that good feeling and knew that he was a prophet of God.

Samuel continued and told the people that there would also be a sign of the death of Christ and that there would be terrible earthquakes and storms and that there would be darkness for three days. Then he again called the people to repent and believe in Christ.

All the people began to talk at once. "He speaks the truth!" said one. "I am going to do what he says. I'm going to find the prophet Nephi and be baptized."

"This Lamanite tells lies!" said another man. "He shouldn't tell us what to do." Many others agreed with him and were angry with Samuel. Tirtza watched in horror as many of these men grabbed their bows and arrows and tried to shoot them at Samuel. She watched others grab rocks and throw them at the prophet standing on the wall.

But nothing touched Samuel.

"See, you cannot kill him!" called a woman. "That is proof that he is a prophet of God. We must believe him." Several more people agreed with her.

But the angry men wouldn't stop. They went to the captain of the guard. "Take this fellow and bind him!" they said. The captain gathered his men and went to the wall. But as they did, Samuel the Lamanite jumped down from the wall and ran, and they could not catch him. Soon the group of people had gone their separate ways.

Tirtza stood by the gate. She was thinking about all that happened there. She must tell her family!

Tirtza ran and ran until she reached her family's land. "Father, Father!" she called. "Come quickly! Temima, Tahlia, Tiva, come quick!"

Soon her family came running. "What has happened?" asked her father, who was out of breath. "Is your mother all right?"

"Yes, yes," said Tirtza. "Sit here. I must tell you what I have heard." She then told her father and sisters all about Samuel the Lamanite preaching from the city wall and all that he said.

"He said five years?" asked her father.

"Yes, he was very clear that Christ would be born in five years," said Tirtza. "Father, I truly believe that this man is a prophet, and we must do as he says."

"I believe he is too," said her father. "We believe in Christ and now we must prepare for His coming. Girls, we must go home now and tell your mother. This is wonderful news."

The family quickly returned to their home, and once again Tirtza told the story to the family and to their mother.

"Five years! Our Savior is going to be born in five years! Just think of it!" said Uriella.

"You believe him?" said Tirtza.

"Yes, I do. I feel the Spirit in my heart when I think of it," said Uriella.

"But it makes me sad to think of Christ's death," said Tirtza.

"Yes, but then He will rise from the dead and come to see us as our prophets have told us," said her father, Amnon. "We will be very old and you will be mothers yourselves at that point. Just think! You and your children and maybe even your grandchildren will see the Christ!"

Tears came to Tirtza's eyes. She would see Christ. And her children would see Him. She knew in her heart it was all true.

And it came to pass that Tirtza was glad she had listened to the prophet. She promised herself that she would do all that he said. She would always repent of her sins and have faith in Christ. And she would always listen to the prophet of God.

LEARNING ACTIVITY: LISTEN TO PROPHET

❋ Have a family home evening where you can pretend to be Samuel the Lamanite. Stand on something like a chair or table and tell your family all the things that Samuel the Lamanite said.

☀ Then have your family read some of President Monson's talks and write down at least one thing the prophet has told you to do. Work hard all week doing what the prophet says.

☀ Read in Helaman 13–15 to listen to all of Samuel the Lamanite's speech to the people. Also read 3 Nephi 23:9–14 where Jesus came to the people and told Nephi, the prophet, that he had forgotten to write down Samuel's words in the scriptures and told him to do it.

DID YOU KNOW?

☀ The name Tirtza means "agreeable."

☀ The people of the Book of Mormon grew many things for food. They grew maize (corn), tomatoes, squash, pumpkin, chili peppers, and avocados as well as many other foods. They would farm the land around their cities to provide food for the people.

Nineteen

UZIEL STUDIES THE SCRIPTURES

A nd it came to pass that Uziel, son of Omer and Naomi, threw his pack into the air. He caught it and threw it up again. He was walking to school and liked to play catch at the same time.

"Whoops!" said Uziel as he stumbled over a pile of sticks.

"Watch where you're walking!" said the old woman leaning on a big stick by the side of the street.

Uziel's face turned red. "Sorry," he said, and he walked away quickly, holding onto his pack firmly.

Uziel was a handsome boy, who was not too tall and not too short. He wore a black robe with red stripes that was tied at the waist with a tan sash. His hair was light brown and straight and tied back with a leather headband. Uziel was a Lamanite, but his family had become faithful members of the Church.

"Uzzy, do you think we'll read some more about Moses today?" asked his little brother. Uziel and his brother went to the church school.

"I don't know—and don't call me Uzzy!" answered Uziel.

"But that's your name!" said his little brother as he walked faster on his short legs to keep up.

"My name is Uziel," he said with a frown.

"Okay, Uzzy," said his little brother, and Uziel let out a sigh.

Soon they were at the school, a small building with many benches inside for the children. He saw his friends and went to sit by them.

"Class, please come to order," said Aviram, their teacher. He was an old man with white hair that stuck up all over.

"Let us begin today by reading from the scriptures. Uziel, please come to the front and read from the writings of the prophet Nephi of old."

Uziel went to the front of the room and opened the scroll that was handed to him by his teacher. He began to read,

"For according to the words of the prophets, the Messiah cometh in six hundred years from the time that my father left Jerusalem; and according to the words of the prophet, and also the word of the angel of God, His name shall be Jesus Christ, the Son of God."

"And read here Uziel," said his teacher, pointing to a verse on the scroll.

He read, "And we talk of Christ, we rejoice in Christ, we preach of Christ, we prophesy of Christ, and we write according to our prophecies, that our children may know to what source they may look for a remission of their sins."

"Thank you, Uziel," said his teacher. "You read very well. Aaron, would you please read from King Benjamin's speech to the people?" A short young man walked to the front of the room and the teacher handed him another scroll.

Aaron read, "And the things which I shall tell you are made known unto me by an angel from God. And he said unto me: Awake; and I awoke, and behold he stood before me. And he said unto me: Awake, and hear the words which I shall tell thee; for behold, I am come to declare unto you the glad tidings of great joy. . . . For behold, the time cometh, and is not far distant, that with power, the Lord shall come down from heaven among the children of men, . . . and shall go forth amongst men, working mighty miracles; such as healing the sick, raising the dead, causing the lame to walk, the blind to receive their sight, and the deaf to hear, and curing all manner of diseases. . . . And he shall be called Jesus Christ the Son of God; . . . and his mother shall be called Mary."

"Thank you Aaron. Children, how long ago did Lehi bring his family to this promised land?"

"Six hundred years!" said all the children at once.

"That is correct. And remember that Samuel the Lamanite told us that in five years Christ would be born. So how long has it been?" asked their teacher.

"Five years!" said all the children.

"Yes, indeed," said Aviram. "Christ will be born soon. And we must watch for the sign of his coming. There will be a day and a night and a day of no darkness."

"But what if he doesn't come?" asked a small boy sitting on the side of the room.

"He will come," said the teacher. "All the prophets have testified that he will be born on this earth. We have many, many scriptures that tell us of Christ and of his coming.

We must have faith, children. He will come to earth soon, and we must be faithful. Now class, it is time to practice our addition. Get out your tablets."

The school day went quickly, and soon Uziel and his little brother were on their way home. Uziel was once again tossing his pack into the air. Bump! He ran right into a large man with a dark blue robe. The man looked down at Uziel with a frown.

"I say that we set a day, and if their big sign doesn't happen, we kill them all," said another man standing beside the large man.

Uziel and his little brother backed away quietly and stood in the shadow of a doorway.

"These believers in Christ will all die," said the large man. "The time for their Christ to be born has past. Let's pick the day right now and if there is no night without darkness and no new star, then they will suffer." The other men in the group shouted in agreement. They argued for a time, and then agreed upon a day.

"Uzzy? What's happening?" asked his little brother.

"Shush!" said Uziel. "We need to get home fast." The boys turned and quietly and quickly went home another way.

"Mother! Mother!" called Uziel as he ran into his home. His mother looked up from the vegetables she was cutting.

"What is the matter, dear?" asked his mother. Uziel told her everything he had heard.

"You must go tell your father everything," said his mother. Uziel ran to tell his father. After he had told him, his father took him to meet with Nephi, the son of Nephi, who was the prophet and leader of the church.

"This is bad news," said Omer, Uziel's father.

"Do not worry," said Nephi. "The Lord always protects those who believe in Him and who are righteous."

Several weeks went by and those who believed in Christ prayed and prayed. And those who didn't believe in Christ were mean and planned for the day when they would kill the believers.

Nephi, the prophet, was very sad for the sins of the bad people. He went out into his garden and began to pray to the Lord with all his heart. Finally, a voice came to him, "Lift up your head and be of good cheer; for behold, the time is at hand, and on this night shall the sign be given, and on the morrow come I into the world." Nephi was happy because he knew that Christ would be born.

As evening came, all the people who believed in Christ

gathered. Uziel and his family gathered as well and stood with them. The bad people also gathered and made fun of the believers.

All the people watched the sun go down. But a miracle happened—it wasn't dark!

Uziel looked at the sky and looked all around him. The sun was down and he could see the moon but the sky was light. He could see everyone and everything just like it was day.

"This is the sign!" called Nephi. "Christ is to be born this day! Repent and believe in Christ!"

All the faithful people who believed in Christ fell to the earth and prayed with joy. And all the bad people also fell to the earth. They knew that this was the sign and they were very afraid because they had been sinning and had refused to believe in Christ.

Uziel kneeled down and prayed. He remembered all the words of the prophets that he had studied. The scriptures were right. Christ was coming to the earth!

And it came to pass that Uziel knew that the scriptures were true. He was glad that he had studied his scriptures and believed in Christ. He knew that it was important to study the scriptures and wanted to study them some more to remember what the prophets had told would happen next to Jesus Christ and to the people.

LEARNING ACTIVITY: STUDY SCRIPTURES

☀ Get your own copy of the Book of Mormon. Get a colored pencil or crayon. Have your mother and father help you find your favorite stories in the Book of Mormon and mark them so you can remember where they are. Have your family help you read at least one verse of your Book of Mormon every day.

☀ Read in 3 Nephi 1 about when Christ was born.

DID YOU KNOW?

☀ The name *Uziel* means "God is my strength."

☀ In the Book of Mormon, the people changed their calendar from the day that this sign was given. They began counting their years from Christ's birth. The Christians in Jerusalem also began to count their years from Christ's birth. The years before Christ was born are called, "BC," meaning "before Christ." The years after Christ was born are called, "AD," meaning "anno Domini," which means "in the year of the Lord" in Latin, another language. This means that that is the number of years after Christ was born.

Twenty

VIDA FEELS REVERENT

And it came to pass that Vida, daughter of Samson and Zimrah, granddaughter of Tirtza, ducked just in time.

"Ha! You missed me!" she called to her sister as the wet rag she had thrown went right over Vida's head.

Vida turned and grabbed the wet rag and threw it back at her sister.

"Well, I won't miss next time." Her sister laughed. "Now come and help me wash these dishes."

Vida skipped over to her sister and bent to help scrub the dinner dishes.

Vida was always skipping or hopping or running. Her mother always said that the girl had never walked regularly a day in her life. She had black hair that was tied in the back. Her brown skirt had a beautiful red and yellow flower stitched in the front and was a gift from her mother. Her mother sewed many beautiful things.

As she scrubbed the dishes, Vida hummed a tune.

"What is that you're humming?" asked her sister Maya.

"A new song I made up," said Vida. And Vida began to sing,

> "*Once a little bumblebee,*
> *Sat down right next to me.*
> *He buzzed and buzzed and buzzed some more,*
> *And then he flew right out the door!*"

"Our famous singer is at it again!" boomed a voice from the door.

"Father!" cried Vida, and she ran to hug him.

"Whoa! You're all wet!" cried her father as she hugged his legs with her wet arms and hands.

"Oh, sorry!" said Vida, drying herself on his cloak.

"You are a silly bumblebee!" said her father, and he picked her up and spun her around. "There, now you're all dry!" he said, setting her down.

"Father, what is the news of the village?" asked Maya. The family lived in the land of Bountiful with their grandmother, Tirtza, not far from the temple.

Their father put down his tools and sat with the girls. "All the members of the church are preparing as best as they can," he said.

"But it has been thirty-three years since Christ was born," said Maya. "When will the sign of His death come?"

"Soon," said their father. "And we must be prepared."

"Prepared for what?" said their mother as she came in from the back room with their grandmother behind her.

"Prepared for the sign of Christ's death," said Samson. "The prophets have told us there will be terrible storms and earthquakes and three days of darkness. How are we coming on our preparations?"

"We have stored food and water and wood," said his wife. "Did you bring the tools?"

"Yes," said Samson. "Now we must pray and wait."

Many days passed. And then one day, the wind began to blow. It became a terrible wind. Samson and Zimrah gathered their children and grandmother Tirtza into their home. They heard shouts in the city and the door of their home began to shake.

"Fire, fire!"

"What is happening?"

"There's a whirlwind!"

Time moved very slowly and then all was quiet.

"Samson, open the door," said Zimrah. "We can't see anything." Samson moved to the door and opened it. All was black. No one could see anything because of the deep darkness.

"It is the sign," said Samson. "Children, do not worry. We will have three days of darkness as the prophets have foretold. We have prepared. So now we just wait and pray."

The days passed slowly. The family could hear the cries of people in the city who were afraid and who were looking for their families and friends. It was a little scary not being able to see anything for so long. They were grateful that they had believed the prophets and had been prepared for the time of Christ's death.

Then they heard a voice, "Wo, wo, wo unto this people." The voice spoke for a long time telling the people of all the cities that had been destroyed and all the wicked people who had been destroyed.

"It is the Lord," said grandmother Tirtza. "Soon He will

come." After the voice spoke, there was quiet in all the city. Then light gradually came, and the family walked out of their home. The city was completely changed. Parts had burned to the ground and many homes were completely gone.

After some time had passed, Vida's family made their way to the temple to worship. Many other people were gathered there and all were still talking about Jesus Christ and about the sign of his death and the voice they had all heard. All wondered what would happen next.

"What is that?" said Vida. "I hear something."

"I don't hear anything," said Maya.

"Listen!"

A quiet voice spoke from the sky, "Behold my Beloved Son, in whom I am well pleased, in whom I have glorified my name—hear ye him."

"Look!" said Vida, pointing up high into the sky. "What is that?"

A man in a white robe glowing with bright light was coming down from the sky.

"It's Jesus!" said Zimrah. "It's Him!" The whole family clapped their hands with joy and stood looking at the sky with tears rolling down their cheeks.

Jesus came down and stood in the middle of the large

group of people. "Behold, I am Jesus Christ, whom the prophets testified shall come into the world."

All the people fell to their knees. The prophets had said Jesus would come, and He was here!

"Arise, and come forth unto me." All the people stood, and one by one, they came reverently to Jesus to feel the nail prints in His hands. Vida walked forward behind her family. Soon she stood in front of Jesus.

He smiled and reached out His hands to her.

"That must have really hurt!" said Vida as she touched the scars on His hands where the nails had been when He was crucified.

"Yes, it did," said Jesus. "But I am all right now." Vida kissed His hands and smiled at Him. He patted her on the cheek.

Soon all the people had touched Jesus and could see that He was real. He had them all sit down and began to teach them many things.

"Blessed are all the pure in heart, for they shall see God," said Jesus. "Keep my commandments." They listened reverently to everything He taught them. He called twelve men from the group, including the prophet Nephi and laid His hands on their heads and gave them the power to preach the gospel and to baptize.

After He spoke more for a long time, He told them He must go. The people looked at Him, hoping that He would stay longer.

Jesus spoke, "Have ye any that are sick among you? Bring them hither."

Vida watched as many people brought their friends and family members to Jesus, and He laid his hands on each one and healed them. The old blind man jumped for joy crying, "I can see! I can see!" She saw her little friend Jonathan who couldn't walk. His father carried him forward. Jesus blessed him, and Jonathan jumped and danced around with a big smile. Many, many people were healed, and Vida watched each one turn and thank Jesus for the miracle of healing them.

"Now, will you all bring your children to me that I may bless them?"

Vida looked up at her father. "Yes, dear, that means you. Go on." Her father pushed her gently toward Jesus. Vida walked forward. Jesus had all the children sit on the ground around him. The children folded their arms and sat quietly.

"Now, everyone please kneel and pray," said Jesus. And He knelt in the middle of the children and began to pray. All the children, even the littlest ones, sat reverently and quietly watched Jesus pray for the people and the children.

When He was done, Jesus sat on the step of the temple and called the children to Him one by one. Soon it was Vida's turn. She went and sat on Jesus's lap and reverently folded her arms and bowed her head. Jesus put His hands on her head and said a simple blessing. Vida had never felt such love and peace and had a warm feeling in her heart. "Thank you, Jesus. I love you," said Vida as she slipped down from His lap.

Jesus finished blessing each of the children. He stood in the middle of them. "Behold your little ones."

Vida looked up and saw angels in white robes surrounded by bright light coming out of the sky. Several angels came and stood around Vida. There was bright light all around. The angels talked to Vida and kissed her on her cheek. Vida looked around and saw beautiful angels around all of her friends. After a time, all the angels went back up into the sky.

Vida was standing on the top step of the temple. She turned toward all the people and began to sing in a clear beautiful voice,

"This day has the Lord blessed me,
A little child of God.

Angels have kissed me,
A little child of God.
Great is my joy!
Great is my peace!
For today I have felt love
Even me,
A little child of God."

Jesus smiled at Vida and took her hand and walked her to her parents. "Your daughter sings with the voice of an angel," He said to them. "She is a precious daughter of God."

"She is," said her parents. "And we love her. Thank you for blessing her and all of us." Jesus climbed back up the temple steps.

"I have waited for this day since I was a little girl and saw the sign of His birth," said grandmother Tirtza. "My father said that my children and grandchildren would see the Christ and we have seen Him. He lives!"

And it came to pass that Vida felt a great reverence for the Savior. She knew that peace and deep love came from her faith in Him. She knew that she would always remember that wonderful day when she had stood in the presence of Jesus and felt of His love for her.

LEARNING ACTIVITY: REVERENCE

※ Every day this week take a few moments to be quiet and reverent. You can do this after you say your prayers, while watching the sun set, and of course during church and Primary! Be quiet, fold your arms, and think about Jesus. You can think about what it would have been like to see Savior, just like Vida. Doesn't it feel good to be reverent?

※ Read in 3 Nephi 11–28 about when Christ visited the people of the Book of Mormon and all the wonderful things He taught them.

DID YOU KNOW?

※ The name Vida means "beloved."

※ The word psalm is the word in the scriptures used to describe a song. In the Old Testament is a book called Psalms that has many songs written mostly by King David. He loved to write songs about Christ. The word "hymn" refers to a song sung in Church. Many of our hymns were written by our Church leaders and other inspired people. Emma Smith, wife of Joseph Smith, gathered many hymns for the first Church hymnbook because the Lord asked her to.

Twenty-One

YARON LEARNS TO BE CHEERFUL

And it came to pass that Yaron, son of Shiblon and Deborah, squeezed his eyes shut as tight as he could.

"I said, it's time to get up, sleepyhead!" said his mother. "It's no use trying to keep those eyes shut!" She wiggled his eyelids and tickled him.

"I don't want to get up," whined Yaron. "I'm tired." He tried to crawl under his blanket some more.

"No way," said his mother as she pulled his blanket off. "It's time to get up right now or you'll be late for school."

Yaron sat up slowly and rubbed his eyes. Yaron definitely

did not like mornings. Actually, he didn't really like the afternoons either, and by nighttime he was ready to be done with the day. He slowly pulled on his clothes—today he would wear brown. He pulled his shirt over his straight brown hair.

"Good morning, Yaron!" said his little sister.

"Quiet, I'm still sleeping inside my body," said Yaron tiredly.

His sister poked him. "You are always such a grumpy lump."

"Am not!"

"Are too!"

"All right, children. It's time to get ready for the day," said their mother.

Yaron ate his breakfast and then walked slowly to school.

"Hey, Yaron, wait up!" called his friend Joshua from the other side of the street. Joshua ran over to walk beside him. "Gee, are you mad about something today?" he said.

"I feel fine," said Yaron.

"Well, you don't look fine. What's with the big frown?" said Joshua.

"I just don't feel like smiling," said Yaron.

As they reached their school, the teacher greeted them at the door. "Good morning, children," he said. "Yaron, are you feeling sick today?"

"I feel *fine*," said Yaron with a big frown.

"Oh, well, I'm glad you're here today. Let me know if you don't feel well," said his teacher.

Yaron had a boring day at school. He didn't feel much like playing and his friends began to just leave him alone. Finally school was done, and he walked home.

Next to Yaron's home was the smithy shop. His grandfather was the village smith and his father worked there as well. They made many things out of metal for all the people in the city. Yaron went inside.

"Well, hello to you this fine day!" said his grandfather. Yaron's grandfather was a huge man with dark curly hair and huge arms. He wore dark clothes with a big black apron covering them. His face and arms were covered in black dirt from working all day. But he always had a big smile on his face.

"Hello, Grandpa," said Yaron, and he went over and sat on a small stool.

"Why so glum?" asked Grandpa.

"Why do people keep saying that to me?" said Yaron, a bit angrily.

"Well, your face looks sad," said Grandpa. "Do you have the Grumpy Lumps?" he said with a teasing smile.

"I guess I do," said Yaron, smiling slightly.

"Well, then, let me just share with you the family's secret cure for the Grumpy Lumps. My grandpa taught it to me years ago, and I taught it to your father," he said. "Now stand up."

Yaron slid off his stool and stood.

"Now every morning, here is what you do. You stand up tall and reach to the sky. Come on, do it with me," said his grandfather as he lifted his huge arms above his head. Yaron felt a little silly, but he raised up his arms.

"Now flap your arms on the side like a bird and repeat after me,

Happy, happy, happy me!
I'm as cheerful as can be!"

Now Yaron was feeling really silly, but he couldn't stop because there was his huge grandpa flapping his arms like crazy.

"Now reach down to your toes and then reach up,
From my toes up to my nose,
I'm filled with cheerfulness, you see!
And pull up your cheeks so your face smiles!" His grandfather had a big, silly grin on his face. So Yaron pulled his cheeks up and then began to laugh.

"See! I told you it works. Gets rid of the Grumpy Lumps every time." Grandpa and Yaron laughed together.

"Now once again!

Happy, happy, happy me!
I'm as cheerful as can be!
From my toes up to my nose,
I'm filled with cheerfulness you see!"

Yaron and his grandfather were really laughing at this point when in walked Shiblon, Yaron's father.

"Ah, I see you're learning the Cheerful Cure!" said his father laughing. And then all three did it together.

"Now I guarantee that if you do this every morning, you will be happy all day long," said his grandfather. "And if you feel the Grumpy Lumps coming on, just flap your arms a bit, and they'll go right away."

"You've learned this just in the nick of time," said his

father. "Tomorrow is the big celebration. We're celebrating two hundred years since Christ came to visit our people."

"Has it been two hundred years already?" said Grandpa. "I remember my grandfather telling me when I was a young boy what his grandfather had told him about Christ's visit. I can still feel the great wonder and love he felt for Jesus."

"It has been a long time," said Shiblon. "And we have truly been blessed. For two hundred years we have had peace and our people have been happy. There have been no wars, no fighting, and everyone has been faithful to the Lord. I am grateful I've been able to raise my family during this time."

"We read about the wars in school," said Yaron. "I'm glad we've had peace with our people."

"Well, it's time we all got some work done!" said his grandfather in his big booming voice.

Yaron loved to help in the smithy shop.

"What are you working on, Grandfather?" he asked.

"I'm making a chisel for the carpenter. Can you get some more wood for the fire?" he said.

Yaron put more wood in the big fire. He watched as his grandfather took a long piece of iron and held it in the fire. The end got very red and very hot. Then he pulled it out with a large glove and put the end on his worktable. He pounded the end of the iron rod with a hammer. Ping! Ping! His grandfather was very strong, and the end of the hot metal rod began to flatten out. He swung the iron rod back into the fire and let it get red and hot again. Then back to the table and hammer some more.

When his grandfather was satisfied, he put the rod of iron into a large barrel of water. Zssst! The rod cooled off, and steam rose into the air.

"How does that look to you, Yaron?" he asked as he pulled it out of the water.

"Looks good, Grandpa. The carpenter will be happy with that," he said.

His father was working on making a fancy metal gate in the corner, and Yaron went over to watch. He loved watching his father and grandfather make so many things out of metal.

"Well, it's off to dinner and bed for you, young man," said Shiblon after a time. "The big celebration will be tomorrow at noon." Yaron kissed his grandfather.

"Don't forget to take your Cheerful Cure with you,"

said his grandfather with a smile. He flapped his arms, and Yaron laughed. He laughed the whole way as he walked over to his home.

The next morning, Yaron squeezed his eyes shut tightly in his bed.

"Time to get up!" called his mother.

Yaron still felt a little sleepy. But just then, he remembered his grandfather's Cheerful Cure. He jumped out of bed and stretched straight up to the sky. Then he began flapping his arms and repeating the words. He felt silly, but he began laughing and laughing.

"Well, someone is happy today!" said his mother as she came into his room. "What's happened to you?"

"I've been cured!" said Yaron. He ran out of the room to eat his breakfast.

His father came in. "Are your chores done yet Yaron?"

Yaron felt a little bit upset. He didn't always like doing chores. He felt a frown starting on his face. Whoops! He remembered what his grandfather said. He flapped his arms and started to laugh.

"I'll do them right now!" he said, and he flapped and laughed out the door.

"What's up with him?" asked Deborah.

"He's been given the Cheerful Cure by his grandfather. I think our grumpy lumpy son is gone!" said Shiblon.

And it came to pass that Yaron was cheerful all day long. He had learned that he could choose to be happy and cheerful no matter what happened to him. He knew that being cheerful helped make other people happy too.

LEARNING ACTIVITY: CHEERFUL

- ☀ Get a calendar and some smiley face stickers at the store. Each day, try the Cheerful Cure in the morning and choose to be happy and cheerful all day long. If you do your best, put a smiley face sticker on that day on your calendar. See how many you can get this month!

- ☀ Read Fourth Nephi to find out how long the peace lasted with all the people.

DID YOU KNOW?

☼ The name Yaron means "he will be happy."

☼ The Book of Mormon people made many things from metal. Nephi said that he taught his people to make things from iron, copper, steel, brass, gold, and silver and that there were many metals in the promised land. It says in Jarom 1:8: "And we multiplied exceedingly, and spread upon the face of the land, and became exceedingly rich in gold and in silver, and in precious things, and in fine workmanship of wood, in buildings, and in machinery and also in iron and copper, and brass and steel, making all manner of tools of every kind to till the ground, and weapons of war—yea, the sharp pointed arrow, and the quiver, and the dart, and the javelin, and all preparations for war."

☼ In Ether they tell about using metal in the promised land as well: "And they did work in all manner of ore and they did make gold, and silver, and iron and brass and all manner of metals; and they did dig it out of the earth; wherefore, they did cast up mighty heaps of earth to get ore, of gold, and of silver, and of iron, and of copper. And they did work all manner of fine work" (Ether 10:23).

☀ The prophets used gold and brass to make square plates like pages of a book to write the scriptures on. Mormon made the golden plates and wrote the whole Book of Mormon on them by etching the words into the gold metal plates so they would last.

Twenty-Two

ZAHARA SHOWS CHARITY

And it came to pass that Zahara, granddaughter of Gili, flipped over the big rock with her stick. Little beetles ran out of the dirt and scooted away. Zahara clapped her hands and laughed.

"Zahara, where are you? It's time for dinner!" called her grandmother.

"Coming, Grandmother!" she called, and she jumped from rock to rock down to the path that led to her home.

Zahara was a short Lamanite girl with black hair that hung in braids. She had dark skin and beautiful big black eyes. She wore a reddish-brown robe tied at the waist with a yellow sash. Her robe had pretty beads around the neck that her grandmother had sewn on. She had made the dress many years ago for Zahara's mother when she was a girl.

Zahara lived with her grandmother in a tall tent called a teepee near Cumorah. Her parents had been killed in the terrible war many years before when she was young and she had been raised by her grandmother.

"Have you checked the fish traps in the river?" asked her grandmother, Gili.

"Yes, Grandma. There weren't any fish, but I'll check in the morning," she said.

Her grandmother nodded her head slowly. "Eat your dinner," she said. After grandmother and granddaughter had finished eating, they cleaned up and sat near the fire.

"Will you read to me?" asked her grandmother.

Zahara had been taught to read when she was young. Her grandmother could not see very well because she was old, but she loved to listen to Zahara read. "What shall I read for you grandmother?" she asked.

"Read to me your mother's stories," the old woman said.

Zahara went to the tent and gathered a few of the stories. Her mother had written many stories about children living in her homeland of Nephi, and Zahara loved to read them. Zahara read until the light of the fire was too dim.

"We must go to bed now," said her grandmother, and they gathered in their teepee.

In the morning, Zahara took the shortcut over the rocks to the river and checked the fish traps. Aha! They had caught three fish! She carefully grabbed the fish out to put in her basket for their lunch. Just then she heard a stick snap.

Zahara turned quickly to her right.

"I'm sorry. I don't mean to frighten you," said a tall man with long golden brown hair.

Zahara took a step back. "Who are you?" she asked.

"My name is Moroni," said the man.

"But you're a Nephite!" said Zahara.

The man laughed a quiet laugh. "Yes, yes I am," he said.

"I thought all the Nephites were dead," said Zahara.

"I believe they are," said Moroni. "I am the last of my people."

"I've never seen a Nephite," said Zahara. "But my grandmother told me about them. Your skin! It is so light. And your eyes are blue! She told me that's what the Nephites looked like, but it sure looks different in person."

"What is your name?" asked Moroni.

"My name is Zahara. It was my mother's name," she answered.

"It is certainly a beautiful name. Where are your parents?" asked Moroni.

"My parents were killed in the terrible war," said Zahara. "I live with my grandmother."

"I'm very sorry," said Moroni. "My father was killed in the war as well. He was Captain Mormon, a very great warrior. The war was a very sad thing."

"So how come you are alive?" asked Zahara as she sat on a rock near the river.

"The Lord needs me alive," said Moroni. "I have a very special job for the Lord to finish His record of my people and the Lamanites."

"The Lord?" said Zahara. "Who is He?"

Moroni shook his head slightly.

"The Lord is our Savior Jesus Christ. He is the Son of God. He came to visit our people—all our people the Nephites and the Lamanites—over four hundred years ago," he said.

"I have heard of this Christ," said Zahara. "My grandmother has told me the stories of the Nephites that believe in him. Was He real?"

"Oh yes," said Moroni. "He lives in the heavens and watches over us—you and me. He loves you dearly."

"How can He if I've never seen Him?" asked Zahara.

"He has seen you because He is the Son of God," said Moroni. "He has given you everything—your life, your body, this beautiful earth to live in," he said.

"Is He the Great Spirit?" asked the young girl. "I believe in the Great Spirit, and I talk to Him."

"Yes," said Moroni. "And you can pray to Him always."

"Would you like a fish?" asked Zahara. "We have caught three and we only need two."

"Why, that's very generous of you," said Moroni. "Thank you."

"Would you like to come eat lunch with us?" she asked.

"I don't think that would be wise," said Moroni. "Most Lamanites would want to kill me because I believe in Christ. I need to stay hidden. But you may tell your grandmother that you talked to me."

"I will," said Zahara. "But would you please come back tomorrow? I would like to learn of this Christ some more."

"I'll try," said Moroni, and he stood, holding the wiggly fish. "It has been very nice to talk to you. I get very lonely. Thank you for being kind to me."

Zahara smiled and bobbed her head and then climbed over the rocks to the path to her home. She told her grandmother all about the strange Nephite she had met.

"I have heard of his father, Captain Mormon," said Gili. "But I did not know he had a son who still lives. He must be very lonely being the last Nephite."

"Grandmother, he looked very poor and hungry. May I give him some things to make him happy?" asked Zahara.

Her grandmother patted her head. "I always said that you have a charitable and kind heart. You love to help others."

Zahara began to sort through the bundles in the corner of their teepee and stacked several by the door.

"Those are your father's clothes," said her grandmother.

"May I give them to him?" asked Zahara.

"They are yours. You may choose," said her grandmother.

The next morning, Zahara jumped out of her blankets. She dressed quickly, braided her hair, and ate breakfast. Then she gathered up her bundles and turned to take the longer way to the river so she could carry them.

"Be careful," said her grandmother. "Not everyone would be happy that you are talking to a Nephite."

"I will be," said Zahara. She carried all the bundles carefully to the side of the river. She stacked them on the rocks and sat and waited. After a time, she saw Moroni coming from down the river.

"Hello, Moroni!" called Zahara.

"Hello, little one," said Moroni, and he sat on a rock near her. "Did you tell your grandmother about me?"

"Oh, yes," she answered. "She said it was all right to talk to you. She has heard of your father. She felt sorry for you being all alone."

"Well, she is a kind woman," said Moroni. "You must get your kind heart from her."

"That's funny. She said I had a kind heart last night," said Zahara. "I just know that I like to help people. It makes me very happy."

"Charity is very important," said Moroni. "Just yesterday I was writing about charity in my record."

"The one you're making for the Lord?" asked Zahara.

"Yes," said Moroni, looking up into the sky. "I wrote that charity never faileth. 'But charity is the pure love of Christ, and it endureth forever; and whoso is found possessed of it at the last day, it shall be well with him.'"

"That's beautiful," said Zahara. "I feel love when I help others."

Moroni smiled.

"What do you write on?" asked Zahara.

"I have plates made of gold," said Moroni. "I carve the words in the plates with a sharp tool."

"That must take a long time," said Zahara. "Why do you write on gold plates?"

"This record must last for hundreds of years. Someday, the Lord will show them to a man who will write the words for your people to read," he said.

"That's amazing," said Zahara. "Can you now tell me more of this Jesus Christ?"

"I'd be happy to," said Moroni. "But I must not stay too long."

Moroni sat with Zahara and told her about Jesus and His visit to their people. He told her about all the prophets and what they had said about Jesus.

"And now I must go," said Moroni. "It might be dangerous for you, and I need to move on."

"But wait," said Zahara. "Look what I have brought you!" She pulled out her father's clothes.

"Where did you get these?" asked Moroni.

"They were my father's," said Zahara. "I want you to have them."

Moroni had tears in his eyes. "This is a great gift," he

said. "Truly you have a charitable heart full of love."

Zahara showed him all the clothes, shoes, and food she had brought him. Tears ran down Moroni's cheeks.

"Thank you, sweet Zahara," he said. "You have given me hope that all is not lost. You will teach your children well. Thank you for these gifts you have given me." He gave Zahara a hug.

Then he gathered the bundles and moved quickly down the riverbank. Then he turned and was gone.

And it came to pass that Zahara felt love in her heart. She felt a new love for Jesus. She knew that having charity for others was important. And she felt a warm feeling and was glad she could help Moroni.

LEARNING ACTIVITY: CHARITY

- ※ Get a small container or piggy bank. Put all your coins in the bank and do chores to earn money to put in the bank as well. Once you have collected a lot, ask your mom or dad to help you donate the money to someone who needs it. You might want to donate it to LDS Humanitarian fund. You can go to their website at LDS.org and find out all the wonderful things they do to help the poor and needy throughout the world.

✺ Read the promise Moroni wrote about how to know if the Book of Mormon is true at Moroni 10:3–7. Then read Moroni's last words to all of us that he wrote on the golden plates at Moroni 10:32–34.

DID YOU KNOW?

✺ The name Zaraha means "to shine."

✺ The Indians (Native Americans) who live in North America and South America are the descendents of the Lamanites who lived during the Book of Mormon. The Lord promised he would bring the Book of Mormon to these people. Joseph Smith and Oliver Cowdery went on a mission to teach the Indians very early in the history of the restoration of the Church. Other people didn't like the Indians, but members of the Church knew that they were the descendants of Lehi and of the House of Israel and are very important to the Lord.

ABOUT THE AUTHOR

Merrilee Boyack is a happy mom to four sons and a grandma to two. She lives in Poway, California, with her husband Steve. She loves to write books and to travel all over talking to people. She also loves to eat mashed potatoes and go camping. Her favorite color is red. Merrilee is a lawyer and serves on her city council. Some of the books she's written are: *Parenting Breakthrough*; *Strangling Your Husband is NOT an Option*; *52 Weeks of Fun Family Service*; *Toss the Guilt and Catch the Joy*; and *In Trying Times, Just Keep Trying*. She is a popular speaker at Time Out for Women and BYU's Education Week, and she is really happy when she's reading books to her grandchildren.

Merrilee would love to hear from you! You can find out more at MerrileeBoyack.com, or email her at maboyack@gmail.com.

ABOUT THE ILLUSTRATOR

Tera Grasser grew up in Litzlohe, Germany. She served in the Wisconsin Milwaukee Mission and received her BFA in illustration at Brigham Young University—Idaho. She is currently working as an inhouse illustrator and graphic designer. Tera has five brothers and four sisters. She enjoys dancing and eating lots of marshmallows. Learn more about Tera at www.TeraGrasser.com.